Did You See That? Too!

Joe Sledge

Did You See That? Too!

Another GPS Guide to the Out of the Ordinary

Attractions in the Old North State

Joe Sledge

Did You See That, Too?

ISBN 978-0-9980968-0-3

Cover Design Barbara Noel and Joe Sledge

This book is meant for entertainment in the form of describing North Carolina's folklore and locations. Some of the stories are based in legend and cannot be verified and the author cannot guarantee their accuracy. Some of these places are on private property or in locations that would be dangerous to access. Do not go unless you have received permission by the correct people, are sure of the legality of entrance, and are sure of your personal safety, or you may face prosecution for trespassing or other crimes, as well as placing yourself in physical danger.

For Michelle, who believed in this, and in me.

Table of Contents

Central

Mountains

Introduction

"I couldn't find it."

That was my lament, and possibly the driving reason for writing this book. When I was researching my first book there was one spot I tried to find early on, the Hattadare Indian Reservation near Bunnlevel, that I couldn't figure out where it was. It was such a curious little place, a tribute and meeting place for members of the various coastal native tribes of North Carolina, with big concrete statues of both natives and lost colonists. I had heard it was run down, maybe a little hidden, and no longer cared for. It was truly a chance for a discovery for me. But since so few people knew about it, outside of probably everyone in Bunnlevel of course, I just didn't know where to find it. It seemed like it was behind the fire department, and it seemed like it would be easy to find. But when I went there, no luck. I couldn't find it.

So I finished my book without it. And for years it preyed on my mind. It was one of those spots that I just had to see. It was kind of legendary. Happily, I figured out where it was, and it had been fixed up, too.

Now, I can write about it and a bunch of other places I either missed or didn't know of. This collection is a little different. First of all, a lot of new places and things have been created in the four years between this book and my first one. And I am happy to see that. I really worried that we may be losing the art of roadside art. Instead I found a whole new group of people preserving all the odd little spots, as well as a lot of people who are really into discovering the same places in which I am interested. It has been a real pleasure to meet fans of the odd like me. What was surprising was just how varied and different my readers and fans were. I figured I would be writing to a bunch of guys who pile into a car and go on road trips for no real reason, maybe some photographers, maybe a few young families who are looking for a stopoff on their trip to the beach or mountains. I ended up meeting retirees who just drive and drive, roadrunners who look forward to a sunny day to put the top down and just go somewhere for a couple hours, curiosity seekers, kids, lots of kids, who just really like the weird stuff I write, historians, anthropologists, teachers, and so many more.

So, I guess it is somewhat appropriate that this book is a little different, too. There still are a large number of just plain weird spots, new or old places that didn't make it into the first book. There are also some interesting little finds that are out in the middle of nowhere, and I think they are important for me to write about, too. Part of my goal was to tell people not only about a place, but to guide them to these spots, and also to tell them if they really need to go there. I don't want my fans to be disappointed. There are a few places that are almost impossible to visit without special permission, "you can't get there from here" type places, starting with the first chapter, the Frying Pan Tower bed & breakfast out in the Atlantic Ocean.

I have also added a nice little feature I first started in *Did You See That? On The Outer Banks*. My Did You See That? Detours are little interludes that list several places to visit in one short chapter. These short paragraphs are what I originally intended to have in my books, just snippets and locations.

Now, you, my dear reader, can go out and make your own stories. I hope they will all be good ones, full of adventure and discovery. I hope you like what I found, and I hope you find some places that will make me extremely jealous.

Oddity

A one to five star rating of just how strange the attraction is. Is it something you can see somewhere else? Or nowhere else? Does it fit in or stick out like a sore thumb? Just how odd, how unbelievable, does this place get? Well, this will help tell you.

★ It makes sense that this is here. I just didn't know about it. These are fitting for the locale, but may be hidden or unknown parts of history.

★ ★ You don't see that every day, unless you live here. Something different, but it still seems like part of the community. It may be less odd than one would think.

★ ★ ★ Whoa, how did they do that? It doesn't fit in, or it has a unique history about it. But, when you learn more about it, it's a little less weird.

★ ★ ★ ★ I hope it doesn't come to life! These are the truly strange stories, places and legends that are hard to believe. It only gets stranger when you discover that the weird stories told about them are all true.

★ ★ ★ ★ ★ I've never seen that before! Now, let's get outta here! These make the visitor truly uncomfortable. Scary, odd, or incredibly different, this doesn't belong, and you are probably not the only one who feels this way.

Difficulty

How hard is it to find the subject or get to it? Can you touch it? Do you even want to? This rating system will tell you how easy it is to find each location. Note that for this book, the Difficulty rating only takes into account how hard it would be to get to the subject if the visitor is already in the area.

★   You can see it from the road. You don't really need to leave the car, if you don't want to. This also includes locations that have easily accessible parking lots.

★★   A little out of the way. This is going to mean a trip down a side road, or a little walking, but you can make it, right? This may include places that are only accessible at certain times.

★★★   Park and walk a ways. There may not be a path. There may be bugs. After all, this is North Carolina. There could be some time issues with a location being available at the right time, such as being open only a few hours a week, or seasonally.

★★★★   Expect to be tired, a little sweaty. Or cold, depending on when you go. These spots may only be accessible for a short period of time. Some people may not want you there. You may need permission to visit or at least a reservation. This is going to be a hike.

★★★★★   You'll need tools, gear, specialized equipment, or the help of others just to get there. You may need permission, and it may not be coming. Going could get you in serious trouble, and you probably should just avoid this unless you are allowed, and you are extremely careful.

GPS Locations and Chapter Layout

The GPS coordinates supplied are approximate, but I have tried to make them as accurate as possible. The coordinates are based on Google Earth maps, as well as handheld GPS units. I suggest you use Google Earth or other mapping tools to find these locations, make sure the coordinates are accurate, and familiarize yourself with the nearby roads and parking areas before going. Also, make sure that these things are still there before you go looking, as sometimes they get relocated, taken away, or destroyed. Some may be in dangerous areas or on private property. Do not go into any area that would be dangerous for you. This book recommends that you always get permission to enter private property before visiting or keep out.

The locations given are either on the actual spot, or on a nearby parking area, if available. I very highly recommend that you keep your eyes on the road as well as the people and vehicles around you, rather than look for these places. Let someone else do the looking. And if you miss it, just keep going and turn around. Never slam on brakes to make a turn, never tailgate or drive too fast or awkwardly. Be conscientious, and courteous. Please realize that one important item about using a car based GPS is that it is made to give directions based on roads. It may try to bring you to a location that is not optimal for parking and walking to a spot in the woods or off a road. Consulting a map beforehand will allow you to be familiar with the location. For some places you may notice a pull off area where others have visited. If you need to, drive around until you find a good place to park and get out. This is why sometimes the coordinates are set for a parking area as opposed to the actual object. Once again, I suggest you use Google Earth as a guide before going.

Most auto GPS devices in North America will automatically put in the negative sign or the West notation for longitude. Online maps will not. When using coordinates on any computer map, use either N and W, or place a negative sign (-) by the longitude. If you do not do this, you end up in Tibet. No, really, you will.

The chapters are essentially laid out from coast to mountains, east to west. But in this book they are also grouped into similar areas, where one location is near the next, as opposed to simply basing the chapters on longitude alone. It may make it easier to visit more spots in one trip, and not miss anything. It may also mean travelers may have to backtrack some if they go into a different area of the state.

Coastal

Frying Pan Tower

Atlantic Ocean 33.48333° -77.58333°

Far out over the horizon, some 29 miles east of Southport, the deep of the Atlantic rises up into Cerulean blue shoals, where the waters of the Gulf Stream mix with the dart of water that was the Cape Fear river. Clear waters and mild climates belie the shallows' ability to reach up and grab unsuspecting ships passing over the shoals. Over the centuries, the shoals have claimed hundreds of ships that have sunk or grounded on the sandbars.

Due to the many dangers inherent in traversing the waters, pressure was brought on the government to protect the sailing vessels of the time. Early attempts to aid in navigation along the Carolina coast were feeble at best. The original Cape Hatteras Lighthouse was so poorly lit, and unreliable, that many sailors would not trust that the light they saw at night was even from the lighthouse. Farther south, the light at Bald Head Island, Old Baldy, built in 1817 to help guide ships into the Cape Fear and Wilmington, was too short and too weak to reach out far enough to direct ships away from the treacherous shoals. By 1854, a lightship would be anchored at the shoals to warn away any wayward vessels. A series of ships would then occupy the shoals for the next 110 years.

In 1964, the lightships would be replaced by a more permanent solution, though permanent will have a somewhat ironic meaning later on. Frying Pan Light, a lighthouse built upon a tall tower embedded in the sand of Frying Pan Shoals, would be built out of sight of land to stand watch over the water and the people that passed over the sandy banks. The tower was built under the plans of a Texas Tower, a platform with four legs driven into the sea floor, similar to an offshore oil rig. The tower served as a home for the keepers, as well as a platform for the taller light tower built into one corner of the site. The flat roofed structure served as a helicopter platform for shuttling people and supplies to and from the light.

Even though the tower served as a more permanent and structurally secure site for the light, automation and the elements would take their toll on the offshore light towers. Soon, the lights could be controlled without keepers, and the locations could be served with less costly buoys or smaller lights. By 1979, the light would no longer be manned. In 2003, the service it issued with its light was replaced with a buoy. Soon after, the tower fell into disuse and disrepair.

In order to get rid of surplus property, the light was auctioned off twice, first in 2009, when the buyer ultimately failed to make an initial down payment, then in 2010, to Charlotte resident Richard Neal. Neal, who lived nearer the mountains than the sea, and did not even own a boat, purchased the light and was able to spend a year rehabilitating the tower. By 2011, he reopened Frying Pan Tower as the most unique of bed & breakfasts.

Now, the tower serves as a rustic inn for those who truly want to get away from it all. The tower is the only thing to be seen from that far out to sea. It offers room for up to 14 guests, with all the basic amenities one would want. There are TVs, Wi-Fi, full bathrooms with showers, kitchens, the works. For recreation, the open top offers a very wide skeet shooting range, as well as buckets of biodegradable golf balls, though the water hazard is probably the biggest any golfer will run into. If it rains there is a pool table inside.

While some may go for the chance to sunbathe on the upper deck, most like the location as a great spot for fishing. The shallow waters and shade from the tower attract all types of fish, just ready for the hook. The tower also serves as a good location for day trips out through the shoals, without the necessity to have to return all the way to the coast.

For a rustic spot, the stay is not cheap. But then, how often will anyone get a chance like this to stay on a light tower in the middle of the Atlantic Ocean? Visitors can choose to take their own boat out to the site, or have one chartered for them. For the most exclusive of trips, a helicopter ride can be arranged for the quick trip out to the light.

Oddity ★★

There were only 6 tower lights of this type ever built, and this is the only one that is open for visiting, or spending the night. If you aren't into fishing, this might be just the spot to write that great novel. Or maybe a really good travel book.

Difficulty ★★★★★

Not only is it a 30 plus mile trip out, by helicopter or boat, once you get there, the time spent may go by slowly unless the fish are biting.

The lightship *Frying Pan*, the last of the many lightships that were used before the tower was built, is still in use. It is a floating bar and grill on the Hudson River in New York.

Ethyl-Dow Bromine Plant

Kure Beach 34.00467° -77.91740°

It may be hard to imagine that a tiny and isolated beach on the southern coast of North Carolina would be integral to the burgeoning desire for the masses to go driving in their new automobiles. Or that it was important to the growth of aviation across the country during the decades after World War I.

But it was the drive of Dow Chemical and the Ethyl Gasoline Corporation to produce bromine in large quantities that led to the building of a large bromine plant on the coast at Kure Beach. At the time, bromine was a much needed element. While bromine was applied in other uses, its primary need was to reduce the knocking of gas engines in cars and airplanes. The bromine would attach itself to the lead in old leaded gasoline, forming lead bromide, which would be expelled in the car's exhaust. Without bromine, deposits would form up on an engine and it would quickly seize up.

FAIRCHILD AERIAL SURVEYS

So in 1933, a small test plant was opened up on Kure Beach, in order to extract bromine from seawater. A plant was built on the intracoastal waterway side of the island, and jetties were extended out into the ocean to collect the seawater. The plant used some of the natural, and unnatural, features of the land when constructing the site. The water had to be collected in a shallow area to warm and be filtered. The plant took advantage of a shallow indentation in the land, a natural Carolina bay, to use as the catch basin for the ocean water. Also, the remnants of an old earthwork built by the Union army in their siege of Fort Fisher were used to shore up one side of the basin as well.

The plant not only functioned well, but it was a boon to the local economy. In 1933, the nation was in the depths of the Great Depression, and any job was a benefit to the locals. Not only did it give construction work to a large workforce, but at its height, the bromine plant employed about 250 people.

The Dow plant functioned from 1934, when construction of the test plant was completed and went online, until 1946, when bromine production was consolidated to the plants Dow had in Texas. During the 1940s bromine was a highly sought after chemical, used for aviation fuel to help the war effort in Europe. Once the war ended, production was severely curtailed.

But during the war, the plant was a highly valued factory, and thus a high value target for the enemies of the U.S. This led to a rather famous legend about the plant and its place in World War II history. Supposedly, the Germans knew the value of the plant so well that it was the target of shelling. The tale goes that a U-boat surfaced on July 25, 1943, at 3:00 am, with the intent to shell the plant. While some believe the story to be nothing more than a broad rumor turned local, as many places throughout the east coast reported being the target of such an attack, this one had the ring of truth to it, according to the witnesses at the time. The submarine appeared in the middle of the night, and as it appeared, a warning went out to all places, including the bromine plant. Normally the plant would continue to operate marginally, with the need for lights and safety around the acids and other chemicals paramount. The lights went out at the plant this time, putting the entire area into darkness. At the same time, an airplane from nearby Blumenthal Field came flying over in search of the U-boat. Witnesses at the plant also stated that they heard the shells whistling overhead in the night. Due to the blackout conditions, the sub had no ability to accurately target the plant. The tale goes on to say that the submarine that shelled the plant was sunk the next day.

While there was considerable testimony to the story's veracity, the tales could be from mixed memories of the events over the many years at war. The coast of North Carolina was front and center at the battles on the shipping lanes of the U.S., and many there saw ships go down in flames to the deadly German boats. Explosions and burning vessels were a common occurrence on the coast, and the U.S. was slow in its ability to respond with the blackout of lights and more active patrols for submarines. It could be that the memories mix the times. By the middle of 1943, the tide had turned for the U-boats. What successes they had in the early years were given back to the depths by American anti-submarine patrols. The research done on this tale pretty much lays waste to the claim that the plant was shelled. While the plant was turned off that night, it was most likely due to a combination of a fleet of ships passing by at night and an erroneous detection of "something" as simple as a school of fish or a passing whale. By this time it was too dangerous for Nazi U-boats to operate off the coast, and the few that went out in 1943 were either used for mine laying or for the safer torpedo runs along Brazil. All the submarines that went out returned during that time, and none had any activity around Kure Beach.

It probably is a good thing that the story is actually just made up, a combination of myth, fear, and mistaken history. But it still makes a great story. If true, it would have been the only time that the U.S. mainland was ever attacked by Germany during World War II.

Even though the plant survived an attack by the Nazis, and the tale survived as well, the plant couldn't survive the peacetime that followed. It shut down in 1946 and production moved to the other Dow plants in Texas. Much of the plant was dismantled for other businesses in the area. But the plant was so well built it survived the demolition. The tunnels and pipes that were used to pull the seawater into the plant remained underground until 2010, when they were finally removed in order to build new houses on the beach. The jetties that stick out into the ocean still remain submerged and are marked with signs at the beach. The remnants of the plant are still there, mostly the blocks and crumbling mortar of a building long fallen down. The place has been visited in the past, and there are some rather unique bits of graffiti there. But there still is a little left to mark an important place in Wilmington's history, and Kure Beach's valuable part of it.

The plant is nothing but crumbling blocks mostly now. It never got shelled. At least not yet. Even though it sits all the way across the water from the big military terminal, it still is in a risky area. The Sunny Point terminal is the largest ammunition port in the world, with cranes loading high explosives onto ocean going ships. While the risk of explosion is almost nonexistent, the base keeps a large boundary around it. The boundary stretches both into the woods as well as all the way over to Pleasure Island, on the sound side. The old plant is on the extreme edge of this boundary. Visiting the old plant is still possible, and permission is granted if the base is contacted in advance so they know people will be over there.

Oddity ★★★

It looks like a bomb hit the place, but really it is just time taking its toll. The remains still define the location, with a rather obvious layout. The tunnels are spooky, and the crumbling walls look foreboding.

Difficulty ★★★★

Not only does this place require a bit of hiking to visit, it also requires permission from Sunny Point Military Ocean Terminal across the water. It's a long walk, and the area is ripe for bugs and critters of all kinds. A winter visit, planned in advance, might be a good choice.

Another popular legend was that German sailors or saboteurs were captured or found dead on the beach, with tickets to Wilmington's Bailey Theater or Southport's Amuzu Theater in their pockets. The implication was that the Nazis walked among the regular townsfolk with impunity in the area. While probably untrue, the rumors may have helped to remind people to keep their secrets to themselves.

World's Largest Rotary Wheel

Wilmington 34.20943° -77.93982°

The Wilmington Rotary Club saw a need for a park in the city and, with typical Rotary drive, set out to create one. In 1945, the local Rotary Club adopted Greenfield Park and began to maintain it. It was simply a desire to clean it up, plant some flowers and do weeding. But when Rotary members get involved, they get involved. Over time, they decided, with, again, typical Rotary passion, to add to the park. In 1965, with the help of masonry students from Williston High School, a school that the Rotarians had long been involved, they built a low wall around the entire park. But not just any type of wall. Visitors to the park will notice the wall is serrated or toothed, like a gear.

When viewed from above, the circular wall looks like the symbol for the Rotary Club. The wall on ground level created a regular pattern of nooks for flowers and vines to grow, with trees lining the inside, all around a central gazebo. It was a pretty nice park. At 240 feet across, it is the largest Rotary Wheel in the world.

Unfortunately, the park and the neighborhood changed over the decades. The area languished, not always cared for, and often the home to drug dealers. It wasn't until two major annual events in Wilmington needed the use of the park that it was cleaned up and restored. First, the Azalea Festival thought that the large Rotary Wheel park would be the perfect place to do refreshments after they had their opening ceremonies. Second, well, let's just say Santa had a bit to do with it.

In 2011, the Azalea Festival wanted an open park to do refreshments on their opening day, and the park space was perfect, even if it wasn't well maintained at the time. So the Rotary Club sprung into action. Rotary clubs are normally known for their passion to a cause, but cleaning up the park actually made the Wilmington Downtown Rotary Club step up a notch. They called the other Rotary Clubs in the area to get more people involved. Each group took many small projects in the park to turn the effort into one big project, cleaning up the drug paraphernalia and graffiti, and planting new flowers in the park.

In addition to the Azalea Festival, the park serves another new purpose. It takes the place of a very old tradition, and another world's largest thing in Wilmington. Long ago in 1928, a town commissioner, J.E. L. Wade, ran a contest to pick a tree in Wilmington to be the World's Largest Living Christmas Tree. Fitting for the locale, a grand Live Oak, the Hilton Park Oak, was picked to be the Christmas tree for the town. For decades it was strung with Christmas lights, and Santa

Claus often sat under the tree to greet kids and learn their Christmas wishes.

The tree at one time stood about 75 feet high, with the creeping branches that are typical of twisted Live Oaks spreading out over 110 feet. It took a serious act of stringing lights to get it to look like a Christmas tree, but Wilmington made it work. Up until the tree finally gave up due to damage from wind and time. The branches couldn't hold the weight of all the wires and lights. For a while a discretely placed pole held most of the weight of the decorations. But soon the tree no longer would work as a Christmas tree. The Christmas tree had essentially died, and needed to be removed. It not only was keeling, it was also in front of the local water plant, and caused a bit of safety issue in that access to the plant was blocked slightly. The tree lighting ceremony was moved to the World's Largest Rotary Wheel in 2012.

So now the lighting happens at the Wheel. The park has become a destination, with an amphitheatre, tall cypress trees, and a beautiful lake as part of the fun. The big Rotary Wheel is a symbol of what Rotary does, a symbol of movement. Rotarians don't like to sit still, always ready for the next production, the next project. Each member is a vital part of the group. They become an important cog in continually moving forward. Maybe the park is just a place for them to rest for a second.

Probably not.

Oddity ★★

The park shape is best seen from the air, but the low walls make it easy to see the cogs of the wheel from the road. The design is deceptively simple, and it's a beautiful spot to stop.

Difficulty ★

There is some roadside parking around the park, but the best spot is across the street at the amphitheatre, where visitors can also take in the lake, as well as a fragrance garden, a popular spot for weddings.

Longest Golf Hole In The World

Carolina Shores   33.91841° -78.61794°

The area of coastal North Carolina, near the southern border, boasts of its seafood so famous it goes by the town name of Calabash. This style of fried fish is tasty and plentiful, and anyone who eats it is going to need a good long stroll to walk off that meal. Luckily, at least if you are a golfer, you have a place to do just that.

Farmstead Golf Links, in nearby Carolina Shores, is home to an 18 hole golf course with a bonus at the end. The last hole on the course is a massive 767 yard behemoth. The hole is so long that it actually starts in another state. Golfers tee off in South Carolina, cross the border into NC, and, if they are lucky, 6 shots later they will have their ball in the hole, or at least on the green. After that many long drives, players probably look forward to a visit to the 19th hole more than most other rounds they play.

Now, technically, this isn't the longest hole in the world. It actually isn't the longest in the United States. It currently is the fourth longest on that list, capped by an 841 yard monster in Virginia. But golfers are probably not the only ones who are glad this hole is not as long as the biggest in the country. Longer holes come with their own set of difficulties. It may be a novelty to have a par 6 or 7 hole as part of a course, but that just adds to the number of sprinklers that has to be installed, the amount of fertilizer used, and the time taken to mow the fairways and greens to emerald perfection. There probably is many a golfer who, upon finally getting to the pin, looked over their shoulder and wondered just what happened to the tee so far away.

Oddity ★★

Walk a (half) mile or so in your golf shoes and wonder how normal this is.

Difficulty ★★

Of course players need to pay a fee and register for tee times at Farmstead, but the public course is open to all players. You will have to walk the entire course to get to 18, and there are several challenging par 3s thrown in to the links course.

Calabash may have been the source for Jimmy Durante's signoff slogan, "Good night, Mrs. Calabash, wherever you are."

Fountain of Youth

Shallotte   33.91423° -78.37284°

South of its namesake town, where the Shallotte River cuts open the white sand shores of Holden Beach and Ocean Isle Beach, the fresh water flows into a soft, brackish marsh before mixing with the salt water on the Atlantic coast. Here at a tiny spot of land, where the marsh grass grows from the shallows, an open spot called Windy Point may be the real home for a spot that has gone into legend over the centuries. Shallotte Inlet may very well be the actual location of the fabled Fountain of Youth.

The Fountain of Youth legend has been in existence for millennia, but gained popularity when it became attached to Juan Ponce de Leon and the early Spanish explorers. The legend held of a natural spring or waters where the ill would be cured, the weak turned strong, and the old made young again. While most of the legends placed the location of the Fountain of Youth somewhere in Florida or the Bahamas, it would be the writer Charles Harry Whedbee that would help reinvigorate the tale at Shallotte Inlet, when he wrote of the legend in his book, *Legends of the Outer Banks and Tarheel Tidewater*. Though he distanced Ponce de Leon from this location, Whedbee described both the waters and the generally healthy disposition of the people who partook of the treatment.

The water of the inlet itself is not the actual culprit in these crimes of wellbeing. It is actually caused by a rather unique type of marsh grass that grows along the inlet but nowhere else in the area. The *Juncus* grasses, a specific type of rushes commonly found in marshlands create a strange milky mold under particular circumstances. Due to the shape and tides of the inlet, and its proximity to the salt water of the Atlantic, the area becomes mixed

with ocean water, and the salt water then creates a mold upon the doughy, breadlike center of the reeds growing in the marsh. At the next tide, the salt water washes the mold off, turning the water a milky white. This is the substance that is the healing water of Shallotte Inlet.

The tales of its healing properties begin with aboriginal peoples knowing of this treatment, but there have been more recent tales of this miracle cure. Hunters and their dogs have been known to take part in the healing waters, along with many locals throughout the area. One story tells of Joseph Huffman, who in 1945 suffered from a degenerative eye disease that left him in near constant pain. When fishing one day, with his eye hurting so bad that he couldn't see to bait his line, he dove in the water for some relief. Upon rising from the water, his eye no longer hurt, and the pain never returned. Huffman began promoting the cure so much that, allegedly, the American Medical Association came down upon him with a threat of practicing medicine without a license.

The tales have continued from the waterway, even into present day. Today people still come to the area to swim, soak, and bottle the waters in hope of a cure all, or even a cure anything. There could be real science in those milky waters, or it could be just a rather wonderful placebo. A visit to the place will be tranquil enough to soothe stressed nerves or a jittery soul. Locals know of the tale, and have no problem with people visiting for the waters. Access is best by hiring a boat or getting a kayak or boat for a rental. The waters can be seen from Windy Point, but access may be difficult, as most of the property is owned with houses on them. There are certain spots where the waterway can be seen. Across the water is a restaurant and small marina. The beach area may have some dangerous tides and currents. No healing water can help a poor swimmer. But boats and kayaks are a good bet for a trip into the calmer bay.

Oddity ★★★

While the rushes grow in other places, and are not local only to the area around Shallotte, they grow nowhere else nearby. And no one can discount the multiple tales of the water healing what ails you.

Difficulty ★★

To actually get out in the water, a boat is needed. Just to see the area is a little easier. Obviously, a dip in these waters in the winter is not advised. A dip at any time should be taken carefully. Don't get in over your head!

Kindred Spirit Mailbox

Sunset Beach   33.85456° -78.53619°

Walk to the end of Bird Island, an empty and undeveloped shore west of Sunset Beach, and see the way a beach looks without all the houses, all the beachgoers, all the interruptions to what nature should look like. The low windswept dunes are covered with the brittle and tough low scrub brush that thrives in the salt air. The beach is smooth, white where it is dry, grey where it is wet. No other footprints dent the shore.

Then notice that there is something out of place on this clean shoreline. At the end of Bird Island, near a bench sitting on the dune, sticks up a black mailbox. You have found the Kindred Spirit.

The Kindred Spirit mailbox popped up out of the sand sometime around 1981. It was exactly what the name implied, a kindred spirit, a friend to listen and understand your problems, your joys, your heartaches and losses, your triumphs and blessings. In the simple, nondescript mailbox sit notebooks full of messages left by other sojourners who made the trek down from Sunset Beach over the years.

The Kindred Spirit was placed on the beach, seemingly mysteriously, long ago. No one at the time knew who put the mailbox up or why. Many people wondered who the Kindred Spirit was. Who read their messages? Who cared for the mailbox and the notebooks inside?

Over time the secret came out. While there were several people who helped care for the mailbox and replace the notebooks, the Kindred Spirit was originally placed there by Claudia Joan Sailor and Frank Nesmith many years ago. Frank met Claudia while she was putting up the box, and helped attach the driftwood post to the box. They often took care of the mailbox, and even replaced or moved the mailbox when it needed repair. But they were only part of the bigger picture for the mailbox, and all that visited. While they put the mailbox in place and replaced the notebooks, there were many others who did so, too. The notebooks were filled, and saved, by many Kindred Spirits over the years. The notebooks are now part of a collection at the University of North Carolina Wilmington, and the visitors number in the thousands.

Over the decades, the Kindred Spirit Mailbox, and its fans, have taken a few hits. When it was first placed, Bird Island was much more of an island than it is now. Care had to be taken when crossing over, as Mad Inlet could become flooded during high tide, and people engrossed in reading the messages could find themselves trapped until the next low tide. And the area is the target of changing coastal water levels, storm surges, and hurricanes. The mailbox has been replaced on occasion after a particularly severe storm. But it always comes back.

There will always be someone on the other end of the mailbox, someone to get the messages and letters posted there. The big step is to get there. The Kindred Spirit Mailbox sits near the end of the island. Parking on Sunset Beach has changed once the new bridge was built. Drive to the end of Main Street in Sunset Beach and park on the side of the road. There are no marked spots, just a grassy median, but it is okay to park on the side. Be sure not to park in or block any driveways. There are marked accesses to the beach. Once you have done all this, be prepared, the walk to the mailbox is about one mile. It will give you plenty of time to think.

Oddity ★★

The Kindred Spirit Mailbox is a very special place for people to share their thoughts, hopes, and dreams. Seeing a mailbox pop up out of the dunes is a very unique sight.

Difficulty ★★★★

This is a long walk from the very end of Sunset Beach. Remember you have to walk back, too. If you go in the summer, be sure to get your sunscreen and water bottles.

Pontoon Bridge

Sunset Beach   33.88289° -78.51316°

It was a rhythmic thing, crossing the bridge to Sunset Beach. A thump of tires dropping onto the bridge, the swift clank clank of going over the metal ramp into the floating pontoon section, the rumble of the car as it crosses the wood planks, another clank as the family car goes down the other side, and the cadenced beat of the bridge sections as the car passes over, closer and closer to Sunset Beach, to the shore, to vacation. The old pontoon bridge was the drummer, counting vacationers in to their favorite song of the summer.

It could also be a beast, a stubborn old sea monster, ready to spoil your day, or eat your boat. It seemed for every car it let over to the shore, it stopped one as well. The pontoon bridge was old, difficult, and a pain for so many. The bridge opened on the hour, every hour, during the day, to let boats through. Which meant that cars were stopped, on the hour, every hour. Kids in the back, hot, screaming, wanting to be there, Dad in the driver's seat, grinding his hands into the steering wheel, Mom hoping they get there before the ice cream melts and the hamburger thaws.

These things and more all began in 1958, when Mannon C. Gore built the bridge over to Sunset Beach. He wasn't really doing anyone a service, nor was he a bridge builder. Gore had bought the land on Sunset Beach in 1955 from former owners the Brooks family and International Paper. In order to develop the land and sell homes there, people needed to get there. So he came up with a simple design that he could build and would work. Mostly. He built a low bridge with an opening section, a creosote barge of sorts on pontoons, which moved on a pivot. A big diesel engine started up to run a winch to pull a cable that moved the floating part of the bridge open and closed. Gore was not really an engineer. More of a guy who got things done that needed to be done. He made the bridge so that there was a road to the beach, where he could sell people property. He also probably used a dredge to dig up a large amount of silt to build a causeway for an elevated road on the island. The things he did back then were things that would never happen today, but it was a different time. He just made things work for him.

Gore needed to get the state to take over the road, and the bridge, which would happen when he sold 50 pieces of property on the island. So he sold the first properties cheap, just to get business moving, and to get out of that bridge. But until then, he was the bridge tender.

Early on, the bridge was open at night to boats. It was more likely to have a boat cruising through the Intracoastal Waterway than a car coming over at night, so the pontoon bridge was left open. Mannon Gore had his house built on the mainland side of the bridge, and he was the de facto evening bridge tender. If a car came over in the evening and had to get across to the island, they simply stopped outside the house and blew their horn until Mannon came out and closed the bridge for them to pass over it.

If someone had to get from the island to the mainland at night, they followed a similar routine, except they flashed their lights as well.

The bridge worked like this. Normally, it was open for vehicular traffic, except on the hour, when it would open for recreational boats. Since the bridge was so low, almost all boats except maybe the smallest rowboat had to wait for the bridge to open. So every hour boats would line up to wait for the opening time. Traffic lights on each side of the bridge would turn red, and gates would come down, stopping all traffic from coming onto the bridge. The bridge tender would then sound a loud long blast on a horn, signaling that the bridge was about to open. Two giant concrete weights would drop on each side, lifting metal ramps that were hinged to allow the pontoon to float up and down with the tide. Once they were clear of the bridge itself, the tender would go downstairs from his perch in the bridge house and fire up a diesel engine. He did it mostly by feel, reaching his hands around the frame of the gear levers, engaging a winch that spun up a cable in the water, pulling the pontoon part away from the rest of the bridge. Finally the boats would be able to get through. But now, the drivers in the cars would sit, and start to simmer.

Waiting for the bridge to close became a pastime for some, an exercise for others, and a frustration for many. People would get out, watch the boats go by, and wonder when the bridge would close. Some would sit, staring back and forth at the red light, the gleaming eye that held them back, occasionally glancing at the cooler or the grocery bags, or the kids getting ready to fight over the back seat space. They were so close, but so far away.

Then the sound came, five quick blasts on the air horn. The bridge was closing. The bridge tender started another winch, another cable pulled the pontoons shut. People hopped in their cars, started them up with a chug or a roar, and hurriedly put into gear, ready to go at the raising of the gates. Probably some father took his time, frustrating his children to no end, with him thinking that there was no need to hurry, it would take a while for all the cars ahead to get going, don't worry, we'll get there. Another flicked his smoke to the road, ground it out with his shoe, before hopping back in. Back in the early days, probably no one put their seat belts on. They just got in and got going.

Yes, there was a rhythm to the bridge and the people that used it. But sometimes the beat got thrown off. The bridge was a simple thing, but it still broke down often. That meant one of two things. Either it was stuck open, or it was stuck closed. Which meant that no matter what, someone was stuck. A bridge repairman had to be called whenever it broke down, and while the fix might be a simple one, it still meant a drive from Wilmington to get there. And a two hour wait for those who were ready to cross. The nearby restaurant, Twin Lakes Seafood, got a lot of business from people who were stuck waiting, but also got a lot of requests to use their freezer to help save those quarts of ice cream that everyone had bought.

Stories abound of incidents that happened because of the bridge getting stuck, or even why the bridge got stuck. One famous tale is of the family that didn't have enough hot dog buns. A father and son were sent over to the mainland to pick up more hot dog buns as they were not sure if they had enough for their cook out. After crossing the bridge to the mainland and getting the buns at the store, they came back only to find the bridge broken, stuck open so that no car could get over. With light failing, the father became desperate and determined. He and his son found a rowboat at nearby dock, piled in, and with all the other vacationers watching and cheering them on, they rowed the boat over to the far shore in order to make that hot dog bun delivery before dinner time came.

Other drivers were not so fortunate. One of the difficulties of the bridge was that it raised and lowered with the tide. If there was a significantly low tide, the pontoon part would be much lower than the rest of the bridge. Sometimes, the pontoon section was too low to move. Sometimes, something even worse happened. One driver had to cross over, or more accurately, down, the ramps and pontoon section, when his truck conked out, right in the middle of the pontoon. Unable to start it, the driver was stranded, as he was surrounded by an uphill push in each direction, impossible for him and others to do. Even a tow truck wouldn't come out, as the dip was so severe that he would tear up his truck. So with no other choice, everyone had to wait until the one lane bridge slowly floated higher and higher until the truck could be moved. The poor driver even got a ticket for impeding traffic.

Boaters weren't immune to the bridge's curses, either. Most boaters knew to plan for a timely escape. They kept an eye on the clock, knowing that they would have to wait an hour if they missed the opening. The bridge would open, and the recreation fleet that was piled up on one side of the bridge would poke through, the bridge tender diligently making notes of each boat's name. Once the line was through, the tender would go through his ritual of starting the engine and engaging the closing winch, pulling a cable to close the pontoon. At low tide, the cable would barely be below the water, and boats, if not careful, could snag the cable, and the obvious trouble would ensue. The cable would break, stranding the bridge open. Of course, it rarely did the boat any good either. One story told of the tender closing the bridge when from far off a fast powerboat, coming at a good clip and doing their best impression of Miami Vice, tried to run the narrowing gap. The cable caught, snapped, stranded the bridge, and wrapped around the go-fast boat's prop, stranding it as well. One person probably got what he deserved, while several hundred got a long delay while the cable was repaired.

These are just a few of the many stories that happened around the Sunset Beach Pontoon Bridge. There probably are hundreds, or thousands, more. Many of them are likely to be somewhat bittersweet reminiscences of the trip over and back, the wait, the way time had to slow down. But the problems of the bridge were just all too real. Plans for a modern overpass began in the 1980s, but were held up over fears that making access to the beach easier would lead to unbridled development, and Sunset Beach would lose its peaceful charm. It took until 2010 for the new bridge to finally be completed. Now access is much easier. The big overpass flies over the water, and cars pass over in about a minute, instead of the long waits of times past. No more one lane roads, no traffic lights telling drivers when they can pass over, no waiting. No melted ice cream.

But it also meant no more slowing down, no bridge stories for many. The dynamic trip to the beach with all the concern and doubt about even getting there was now a thing of the past.

Fortunately, there were some people who decided to preserve those memories, and their root cause. The pontoon section of the bridge, along with the metal ramps and the bridge tender's building, were picked up by crane and placed next to the new flyover. Cars can no longer go over the bridge, but people are free to park and walk over the bridge. The upper part of the tender's building is now preserved as a museum. Using photos from before the building was moved, the interior was restored with its original furnishings to a near identical setting. The lights and siren control board is still there, and visitors can even go through the steps of opening the bridge, sounding the siren in the process. Fortunately, starting the old dirty diesel engine is no longer part of the process. A visit to the downstairs will lead visitors to a small gift shop, where fans can get more positive souvenirs of their trips over the bridge.

The Old Bridge Preservation Society even offers events around the bridge in the summertime. There are visits from local beach animal rescues, history lessons, visits from the fire department and police, arts and crafts and more. Sunset Beach offers a quiet beach visit during the day, and the old pontoon bridge gives families a chance to get away for a while, and enjoy a change of pace for kids and adults alike.

So now travelers are no longer forced to stop at the bridge. Happily, they can simply choose to. Parking is right next to the bridge, in an unpaved lot. Walk up on the bridge and imagine the sounds, the cars crossing the ramps, the rumble over the wood...

Oddity ★★

It actually is rather strange to see a bridge, even a part of a bridge, over land and under trees. But there is a nice sense of joy in visiting, hearing the old stories, pretending to be the tender, and watching the boats pass by.

Difficulty ★

The bridge is just off the road, with a well-marked sign and good parking. The museum and gift store may have limited hours based on seasons and time of day, but seeing the bridge is possible at any time.

Fort Apache

Supply 33.95000° -78.25683°

"Vistors Welcome"

Yes, "Vistors" are welcome, so are visitors, company, and guests.

There is a reason why a welcome sign is prominently posted outside Fort Apache, a combination scrapyard and backyard town on Stone Chimney Road near Supply. Passersby will be really impressed, a little stunned, and probably unsure about whether or not it is okay to stop by and visit. Even after they go in, they still may not be sure.

Fort Apache is the creation of scrapyard dealer and collector Dale Varnam. After a colorful and furious life in the 1980s, Dale founded his variety town as a way to display, and occasionally sell, the strange menagerie of items he had collected over the years. Don't let the wild entrance with its funny signs and strange homemade cars fool you. While there are certainly a lot of items, things, whatevers, inside, the place is in a rather orderly design. The walls encase a vaguely western style town, with the different store fronts one might expect in a cowboy town. There is a drug store, liquor store, general store, court house and funeral parlor, just to name a few. And while it does have that western town feel, the closest you will come to horses will be an old Ford Mustang in the middle of the dirt road.

Not that there aren't animals there. Dale has a brood of chickens wandering the place, along with a turkey, and a cat or two. On the inanimate side, the place is scattered with toilets, mannequins, and homemade sculptures of Dale's creation, strange figures made of car parts scavenged over the years. Dale seems to like cars. In addition to the Mustang, he has a nice Herbie the Love Bug replica and a few old police cars. Some he has decorated with drivers and passengers, so don't be surprised to see someone sitting in the cars.

Describing the place is difficult. It really just has to be seen. The big thing to remember is that there are a lot of strange things to be seen, and some of them may raise questions. To be delicate about it, the best explanation is this description of Dale. There was an old Dale, and now there is a new Dale. Old Dale did some stuff long ago, and he now does stuff to help make up for what happened in years past. So, yes, there are signs and cars and even a bus with drug references on them. Dale now does a lot of work to help keep younger people off of drugs, and is an informal mentor of sorts. Much of the money he raises from his scrapyard and his collectible sales goes to helping needy families in the area. Dale even throws a wild Halloween party every October to help raise funds for charitable needs.

Dale's collection is eclectic, to say the least. Not only does he have a lot of antiques, scrap, old cars, and the ilk that one would expect, he also has gathered a large amount of movie and theater sets. Many of the sets of traveling shows for live plays have ended up there. He even ended up with a few rare pieces from The Wizard of Oz in his collection. Because he has such a large and varied amount of decorations, Fort Apache has become a popular place for photographers. Fort Apache hosts fashion shoots as well as allowing amateur photographers to come and practice their craft. It even has appeared in film, as a backdrop in the movie *Don't Know Yet*.

Dale has also appeared on film. Well, video. Fort Apache was visited by Mike Wolfe and Frank Fritz from American Pickers to see just what Dale had inside those walls. Considering the size, and the strangeness, of the place, they probably didn't scratch the surface of his collection.

Visiting Fort Apache is pretty easy. It is usually open every day during the day in summertime, and after Labor Day weekends are a good time to go by.

Oddity ★★★★★

Look, this place is just weird! The reason that the description to Fort Apache is so vague is because it really is extremely difficult to describe. In addition to the anti-drug references, there are quite a few signs that may be considered misogynistic. Some things might be uncomfortable to explain or show to little kids.

Difficulty ★

Parking is right off the street, and it is open until 5pm all summer, and weekends the rest of the year. Right on Stone Chimney Road, drivers will only miss this if they are going too fast.

Three Sisters Swamp

Ivanhoe   34.49731° -78.24522°

A lone hunter crouched in the tall grass of the coastal flatland, still in the fading light of dusk, waiting for a deer to cross his path while heading toward the tender leaves and water that came from a nearby slow moving river. The grass grew well, and deer were plentiful at the time. It had been a warm summer and fall, with light rain falling occasionally, keeping the ground damp, but not muddy. It allowed for easy tracking, and also kept his footsteps quiet in the twilight. He would be successful in his hunt, taking a doe back to his hunting band, and back to his tribe that settled nearby. This would be good ground for a while, with good fishing and hunting, as well as natural resources that would support his nomadic tribe until they moved on.

Little did he know what was happening nearby in the swampy marsh. An insignificant event would occur, but one that needed just the right timing and environment to take place. A bald cypress would have its seeds thrown from a small cone. The seed needs just the right type of personal climate to survive. Many get eaten by squirrels or turkeys, but this one escapes to fall to the earth. It may be carried by floodwaters downstream, or it may find purchase nearby. No matter where it ends, the seed needs to be out of the water. It will not germinate in the tannic tea that courses through the river. Nor will it take root in dry soil, or even well drained wet loam. It needs a very special ground to find its roots. The earth needs to stay damp for months for the seedling to sprout. Then it must hurry on with its work, growing quickly to stay above any floodwaters that may come. This seedling will do just that, reaching up to the sun quickly, taking hold and making a small island in the swamp where it is born.

The year is 364 A.D., and the birth of a bald cypress that will be known to some as BLK69, to others as Methuselah, has just occurred.

Three Sisters Swamp is the home to BLK69, though neither the swamp nor the tree were known as that at the time the tree first sprouted. Three Sisters Swamp gets its name from a spot in the Black River where the stream nearly runs dry and feeds most of its water into the swamp. Three intertwining channels course through the area, giving the swamp its familial title. The Black River is a picturesque dark water river that runs through Sampson County and dumps into the larger Cape Fear River. Its waters benefit from the lack of pollution along the sides of the river, making the water especially clean. Its brown tea color comes from the natural detritus of leaves and needles that fall into the water, turning it into a mildly acidic coffee color, flowing over a soft white sand bed in places. Because of the river's natural state, it has long been a great place for the ancient cypress trees to grow and flourish. In 1994, it was designated an Outstanding Resource Waters, giving the river even more protection.

Due to the distinctive nature of the river, and the age of the growth in the swamp, the trees there lend themselves to scientific study. In 1986, while North Carolina was suffering from a two year drought, professors of geosciences from the University of Arkansas Dr. Malcolm Cleaveland and Dr. David Stahle came to the swamp to get core samples from the old trees to study the periods of drought and flood that had happened over the centuries. Tree rings can show periods of drought by a tighter grouping of rings, as they grow more narrowly than in wetter seasons. The professors canoed into the river and its swamp with the rewarding old growth trees in order to gather their core samples. Once there, they realized that the swamp was probably the best collection of old growth cypress ever found. They spent their time coring and tagging trees, gathering the information the rings would provide. On their last day, one tree drew their attention. It was big, certainly, but more importantly, it was solid.

Cypress trees grow big, wide and tall, but they can often hollow out on the inside, leaving shadowy shelters sometimes big enough for a person to get into. When this happens, taking a core doesn't help much, as all the interior rings are gone. But the tree they found, number 69 of about 75 trees, was solid through and through. Dr. Stahle climbed 20 feet up the tree to get to where the trunk was more uniformly round in order to take a good sample. Upon observing the core, they knew they had an incredibly old tree, at least 1,700 years old. Tagged BLK69, Methuselah was discovered.

Over the years, the tree would become legendary, not just for its size and age, but also as a sort of Holy Grail of the kayaking world. Getting into Three Sisters Swamp is not an easy task. Once the Black River reaches the swamp's waters, the river path dries up, only flooded at times of high water. The rest of the water feeds into the swamp and its labyrinth of creeks, trees, and cypress knees. Getting around in a kayak often includes trudging in shallow water, pulling the boat behind the paddler, as the giant knees that stick up from around the cypress trees can be nearly impossible to pass with a kayak and paddle.

But many people will attempt to pass through the creeks and bends to get to the swamp, and they are rewarded with some amazing sights. The cypress there are enormous, and the knees, the pointy roots that stick out from under the water, can grow to six feet. The purpose of the knees is still unknown, but they may provide a buttress to hold the tree up in high winds or in challenging soil, or they may work as a barrier to keep other trees from competing with the cypress. Either way, they are ever present in the swamp.

Finding Methuselah has become quite the challenge to many kayakers. Once they gain entrance to the swamp, finding the exact tree is difficult. The tag that was originally placed on the tree has probably long since fallen off in the intervening decades, and another tree has received the same tag at some time. Some explorers have been able to distinguish the tree from others in the swamp due to some distinctive characteristics, a distinguishing lean, and a rather large burl or knot about ten feet above the water line.

Finding Methuselah is a challenge, as is getting into the swamp, but the prize is worth it for the kayakers that pass through. There are several put ins for kayakers a few miles upriver from the swamp, and there are also guide services with kayak rentals available for people new to the river, or to the sport. There are several public and private docks to put in a kayak. Some will have fees, and parking may be limited. But once you get out on the water, time will slow down. You may even find yourself going back in time, some 1,700 years or more. Enjoy the trip.

Oddity ★★★

The cypress trees that grow in Three Sisters Swamp are distantly related to the giant sequoias that grow throughout California. Though lacking in height of those giants, the cypresses that grow here are still immense around the base. Add to that there are trees that existed before English was even a language makes them all the more rare.

Difficulty ★★★★★

Getting to the Three Sisters Swamp is difficult to say the least. Places to put in include at the bridge on Beatty's Bridge Road, Hunt's Bluff Wildlife Landing, near Kelly, and the NC Wildlife Landing in Ivanhoe. There are also private landings where you can put in for a fee. Once in the water, expect to spend the whole day, and expect to do some paddling. Getting wet is a given, as is the occasional bug bite. And navigating the twisted braids that give the Three Sisters its name is no easy task. The best advice is if you want to go, go with a guide.

The trees in Three Sisters Swamp may be older than the 1700 years that BLK69 was dated. When taking the core, Dr. Stahle had to get above the misshapen base to get a straight line, and even then he missed the center of the tree. It most likely is older than its given date. Other trees may be even older than that. Since they are hollow on the insides, but still alive and growing, the largest trees could have been around for more than 2000 years.

Phillips Island

Beaufort   34.73183° -76.68632°

Menhaden is certainly an unremarkable fish. Unattractive, bony, and oily, it is not one for the dinner plate. It does serve other more useful purposes. The fish is plentiful. So much so, that the name itself seems to sound plural. One rarely refers to menhaden in the singular, a menhaden. These fish exist in gigantic schools, swimming close to the surface in groups as big as a football field. The schools are so big that from the air they resemble more a shiny oil slick than fish. In the food chain of the sea, menhaden are an early link. They eat plankton, and everything eats them. Menhaden are a popular food source with game fish. Mackerel, bluefish, and tarpon love the menhaden.

While humans don't eat the menhaden, they do serve other purposes. The fish can be used for meal for animal foods, and the bone meal is also useful in fertilizer. Way before colonists first arrived in the New World, natives used menhaden as a way to nourish the fields. The name even comes from a Native American word meaning manure. Even today, menhaden are fished for their oil to use in Omega-3 supplements.

That's why for decades fishing for menhaden was a prolific occupation. In Beaufort and Morehead City, menhaden fishing was a major source of income for over 100 years. After the Civil War, and especially after the 1890s, menhaden fisheries were huge in the area. People came for the hard, backbreaking work, from May through January. Boats would go out, looking for the schools of the shiny fish, then send out smaller craft to circle the schools, surround the fish with nets. The nets were pulled up by hand, dozens of men gripping the mesh until their fingers turned to claws, often unable to open their hands from the death grip of the cold, wet nets even after they went to shore and had gone home. It was unbelievably hard, laborious work, and would even take the life of a fisherman from a heart attack due to the stress and exertion.

But the fish came in, and the money went out. Caught by the ton, the fish were brought back to Beaufort. That's when the most noticeable part of the menhaden fishing occurred. The smell. The fish were processed in giant factories, the fresh caught fish going into steamers, having the water and oil pressed out and separated, the rest of the fish pressed into cakes to use as fertilizer or feed. The oil is used in paint, soap, linoleum, and omega-3 supplements.

So menhaden were the fish to be caught around Beaufort for about a century, a smelly cash sea cow of sorts. It wasn't until tourism and sport fishing in the 1980s grew in the area that menhaden started to go by the wayside. Visitors didn't like the smell, and sport fishers didn't like the loss of a major bait fish. With fewer menhaden in the water, game fish like king mackerel and tarpon would have less to feed upon. Soon there was a battle between the sport fishing industry and the menhaden fisheries. The little shiny fish stood no chance against the bigger, more glamorous catches.

By 2005, the last menhaden fishery was closed, and later torn down.

But there are still remnants of the great industry, right in the waterway near the seaside towns.

Phillips Island sits just north of the bridge between Morehead City and Beaufort. Visible clearly from the water, a low chimney rises up from the sandy beach and scrub grass of the island. Newport Fisheries opened the plant on the island, and it passed through several owners. The plant may have gone out of business in the 1930s, but no one is entirely sure when the plant operated. Llewellen Phillips bought the plant and island in 1932, and it may have been in operation at that time, but it had not been working in most residents' memories. In September of 1953, the plant caught fire and burned. The flames were so bright that hundreds of people from the town came out to the causeway bridge to watch the place burn. The only things that survived the fire were the tall brick chimney, a large gear that sticks out from the base of the stack, and a few rusted iron buckets used to cook the fish.

Now the chimney sticks up out of the island like an unlit beacon. Phillips Island has small soft white beaches, and a small cove. Most of the island is short marsh grass, but there are some taller scrub trees that grow around the chimney. Long ago the large menhaden fleet passed by. Now only kayakers and sport fishing boats cruise the waters. But the island is not uninhabited. For decades, the island has been a landing spot for white heron and other wading seabirds. Visiting the island, people may see flying white clouds of the birds, circling the green and white island, floating on a sea of blue.

Oddity ★

Most of the islands in the Intracoastal waterway are nearly flat, with only short grasses as a natural crew cut to the sandy shore. This one has its own smokestack.

Difficulty ★★★★★

You'll need a boat, obviously. Also, good weather, and be in decent shape to sail, or paddle over. And to get back, because there's no place to stay, and that chimney isn't very safe to be near, with a big hole in the bottom of it.

While menhaden is the correct name for the fish, most locals refer to it as shad. It is also called pogey and bugmouth.

Phillips Island is owned by the Phillips family, and as of this writing, is for sale. The price might be good, but there's no power, no water, no sewer, no roads to get there. But still, there is a St. Phillips Island near Beaufort, SC that costs a little more. Owned by Ted Turner, it has a private house with solar and generator power, and a water tower for running water. He's asking a little more, at around $34 million.

King Neptune

Morehead City 34.71955° -76.71281°

When the ocean waves pump and pound the shore, we often say that Old King Neptune is kicking up some stormy seas. King Neptune was more likely off fishing in a stream. Neptune was the Roman god of waterways, rivers and streams. His wife Salacia was the goddess of the sea and salt water.

So it probably was good placement for a King Neptune statue to be placed along the Intracoastal Waterway. Neptune guarded the water and the Channel House Restaurant until the new bridge at Atlantic Beach was built in the 1980s. He found a new home at the Olympus Dive Center. It was started in 1975 as a charter dive business by the pioneering diver Captain George Purifoy, who discovered shipwrecks such as the German submarine *U-352* and the *USS Schurz*.

Today King Neptune protects divers as they head out, keeping the waterways calm, and attracting a bit of attention for himself on the docks. Nearby is a deck gun salvaged from the U-boat discovered by Purifoy. Neptune has no need for it, of course, as long as he has his trident.

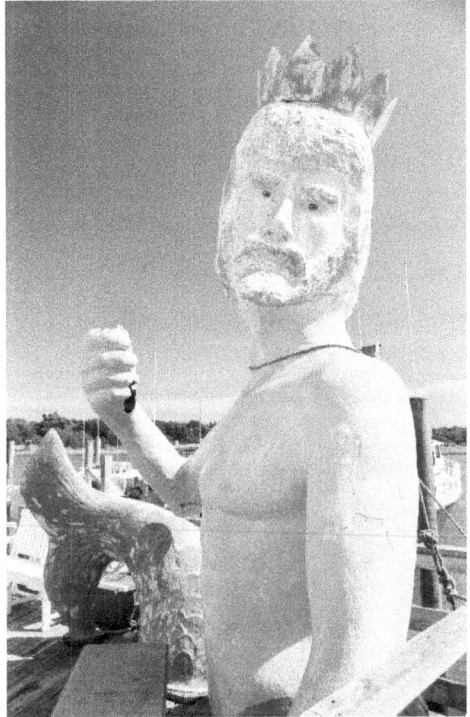

Oddity ★★★

He comes up out of the deck, his fish tail swishing behind him, eying everyone that plans to look out over his waters, as if to make sure they are worthy to pass. Maybe offer a fish sandwich to him in tribute. Nah, eat that thing!

Difficulty ★

He is on the side deck of Olympus Dive Center. A good view is from the walkway to the side. Just stay out of the way of divers hauling gear and don't fall in the water. Neptune would just laugh and laugh.

Salvo Post Office

Salvo   35.54530° -75.470718°

The villages south of Nags Head grew up on the sandy banks that the Algonquin called Chicamacomico, "the sinking down sand." Three small towns, Rodanthe, Waves, and Salvo grew out of small settlements along the coast. As they developed and grew, the towns took their own unique names. Rodanthe was possibly named after a flower, and Waves was taken simply because it was no longer South Rodanthe, and chose the name from the continual gifts from the ocean.

Salvo got its name more curiously. Originally known as Clarksville, it was not even a mark on a map. During the early battles of the Civil War, a Union warship passed by, and a sailor noticed the settlement. Even though it wasn't marked, the captain ordered that they get a salvo, a blast from the ship's guns. A sailor noted the location with the words "salvo", and an arrow pointing at the spot on the map. The name stuck, and when it came time to build a post office, a sure sign of having arrived as a town, the area became Salvo.

And what a post office they got. Built in 1910, it was only 8 feet by 12 feet. There was little more in the shack than a lobby and a small workroom. People would enter, receive their mail, and turn to leave. While it may have seemed strange to have such a tiny post office, it actually made sense at the time. The area was sparsely populated, and it was easy for a single postmaster to handle what mail came in and out. The building could be moved from place to place, as a new postmaster would take the job from a retiring one. The building would sit in front of the postmaster's house, making the commute to work an easy one.

For about 80 years, the building was a small landmark. It was considered the second smallest post office in the nation by the US Postal Service. Sadly, in 1992, the original post office was burned by an arsonist. It was rebuilt in 1993, and placed on the national register of historic places. The post office is no longer used as such, but it still has 94 boxes inside.

Oddity ★★

It's cute enough for a post card.

Difficulty ★

The post office is small, but it's just off the main road of Highway 12, next to the fire department. Don't forget the zip code.

Cora Tree

Frisco   35.26128° -75.59113°

The twisted oaks that cover much of Hatteras Island are a pretty common sight throughout the many communities there, but no other tree has a story quite like the Cora Tree, which sits in the middle of the road in a housing development in Frisco.

The Cora Tree has a legend tied to it, the type of legend that that is often told throughout the Outer Banks, but this one has a twist. More about that at the end, just so the surprise is not ruined.

Sometime in the 1700s, in one of the quiet fishing villages that dotted the Hatteras coast, there was a strange, mysterious woman named Cora that lived in an old shack in the soundside forest. She lived only with a small child, a "knee baby," as often called in the legend. Both woman and child were peculiar. Cora and her child lived alone, with no man ever appearing at the house. The child did not act like a typical toddler, but always stared at others with a peculiar frown. But the people of Hatteras were at least tolerant of peculiarities, if not accepting of her strangeness. They paid her little mind, and gave her a wide berth, leaving her be for the most part.

Strange things occurred on the occasions she appeared, though. The local fishermen knew the vagaries of their profession. Days may be good or bad, and no matter their skill, there may be a trip out to sea where their nets would come back empty. But Cora always seemed to have plenty of fish. Once, when walking by a cow, she brushed up against it, and the cow went dry, never to give milk again. And most peculiar was when a boy of the village taunted Cora's baby, only to come down with a fever that night and almost die. Many suspected her of being a witch, but rather than cause more problems, the local islanders just gave her some extra space.

Had Cora lived in the north of the country at the time, like in Salem, Massachusetts, she would not have had an easy time of it, but living in the more tolerant southern coast, it took an act by a displaced and displeased visitor to bring things to a head. Shipwrecks were a common occurrence, and brought the human flotsam along with any broken ship with it. In this way, Captain Eli Blood and his band of freed slaves from Barbados found their way to the coast of Hatteras. After his ship foundered on the shoals and broke apart, the captain and crew were made guests of the island until help could come from up north to save what was left of the ship's cargo, as well as rescue the crew. Captain Blood made his home as a guest of one of the many fishing boat captains while his crew happily pitched camp under the ships' sails on the beach. The balmy days and beautiful beach made for relatively easy, if boring, living for the seafarers.

Captain Blood in due course learned the story of Cora the witch, but aside from some Puritanical grumbling, it does not seem like he did anything about it. That is, until a young man, an upstanding and highly regarded member of the village, was found dead on the beach one morning. Flat on his back in the wet sand, his hands were clasped together at his chest, and the number 666 was burned into his forehead. His face was a rictus of terror. There was no evidence of the cause of death, but a set of footprints led away from the body, into the woods. The tiny prints were the match of a light woman, and quickly, suspicion turned to Cora.

Captain Blood rounded up his crew and went to Cora's shack to capture and question her, as only a Salem preacher would. Cora was bound, hand and foot, and prepared for her first test. Knowing that a witch would use her magic to save herself from drowning, Blood and crew threw her into the calm shallows of the sound, only to find that she floated. Captain Blood, a self proclaimed witch hunter, felt that proved her to be a witch, for if she was human she surely would have sunk and drowned. Blood took no mind that the sound water was not deep enough for just about anyone to drown. He then pulled Cora from the sound, and proceeded to his second step. Drawing his knife, he attempted to cut her hair. His blade found it impossible, and he declared her hair to be like wire. Finally, in an attempt to divine truth from the spirit world, Blood and his crew all cut their fingers to drip blood into a vessel of water, stirring it until it foamed. Peering into the murky sanguine mess, they all stated they saw Cora, conversing with the Devil himself.

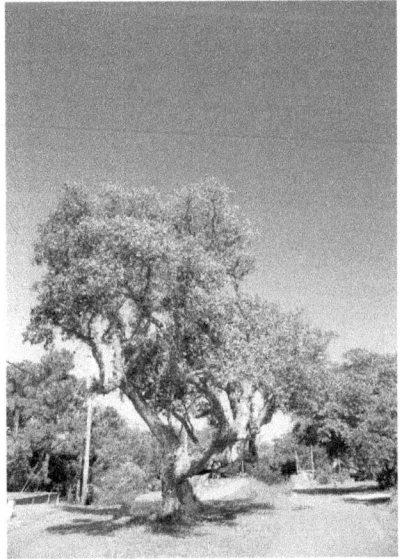

Thus proven, at least to their satisfaction, Blood took action. The townsfolk were aghast, but dreaded interference in the profane actions for fear of the wrath of either Blood or Cora. Captain Blood and his crew tied Cora and her child together, bound to a large live oak tree. Then they gathered kindling to place at her feet. One of the townspeople cried out for him to spare the child, but to no avail. Blood was set to his task. At the last moment, as Blood approached with a lit torch, one man tried to stay his hand. Captain Tom Smith pleaded with Blood, stating that whether or not she was a witch, she should be tried in the courts for the murder, not killed this way. As he said that, he heard gasps from the crowd. Cora's child began to hiss and spit, and the babe transformed in front of their eyes into a ferocious wild cat. With this act, all intervention by the townsfolk stopped.

But another intervention was occurring at the same time. Clear skies became inky black, as a thunderstorm roiled in the atmosphere. All the spectators, sailors and local alike, looked on in wonder. Captain Blood, his spine stiffened, approached Cora and her familiar to light them afire. Before he could approach, a giant bolt of lightning crackled out of the sky, striking a cacophonous blow to the tree.

The entire group were knocked down, stunned by the shock. When they finally recovered, shaky from the experience, they all noticed the smell of sulfur in the air. The tree had been struck, and was split down the middle, smoking from the bolt. But, mysteriously, Cora and her cat had disappeared. The ropes were still tied tight around the trunk of the tree, but Cora and the wild feline were gone. The tree was burned down the middle, smoking and split.

The story ends at that point, except for one little item. The tale seems odd, just a legend, right? It hardly can be true that this occurrence actually happened, except for one thing. While there was no trace of Cora or her familiar, there was one mark left after her disappearance; the name CORA was carved into the tree, burned into the trunk, as if by a fiery pointed finger, a reminder of who had been there and what had happened. To this day, the letters can still be seen in the tree.

Oddity ★★★★

The tale is pretty weird just in general. What's really strange is that the letters have stayed in the tree, never grown over. What's even stranger? Cora's wild cat, a strange furry beast with piercing green eyes and a deep red mouth, so unlike the usual witch's black lap kitty, has been seen over the years in many parts of North Carolina.

Difficulty ★★

The tree is on Snug Harbor Drive in Brigands Bay down in Frisco. With the story so legendary, but with the twist of the letters carved in the bark, many people go by to see it. You will have to go to the tree to see the letters, but maybe don't touch it...

The Captain Blood of this story is referred to as Captain Eli Blood by Charles Harry Whedbee in his book *Blackbeard's Cup and Stories of the Outer Banks*, the book that made the story famous. Captain Blood does not seem to have a relation to the novel character Captain Blood or any pirate captains, and seems to be a respectable, if overzealous, ship's captain. While made out to be vicious, it should be pointed out that Captain Blood did turn out to be right, and Cora actually was a pretty evil witch in the legend.

Corolla

A Did You See That? Detour

Corolla once was the end of the road for the Outer Banks. Past Corolla was a near no-man's land. A desolate flat beach that was the denizen of only the wild ponies and a few hardy four wheel drive vehicles. It was rumored that trees grew from the ocean, and buffalo roamed wild near the border of Virginia. Dunes and scrub brush rolled over the land, with only the old lighthouse peeking above the tree line like a lonely candle in a storm.

But the land was there, and it called to the people to come. So they did, by the thousands. Houses were built and bought, vacationers came, and with them came the development of Corolla. Better roads and more houses, stores opened, and the old lighthouse and the hunt club were preserved. It was no longer the desolate Atlantic Flyway meant only for the birds and the hunters that sought them in the dead of winter.

Today, Corolla is another destination of the Outer Banks. The road may still end there, but that hasn't stopped people now. Farther north in Carova, giant houses reach up to the sky, though they are built on sand. No paved roads go there, but there are still plenty of paths in the sand. Penny's Hill is a popular spot to picnic and drive. Its smooth flat bowl turns into a parking lot for a lot of off road vehicles in the summer. Corolla developed its old historical spots into destinations, and found its wide smooth beaches to be a big draw with visitors. Now there is much more to see on the northern beaches than before.

Kill Devil Hills Lifesaving Station

36.37887° -75.83036°

It might seem weird to find the Kill Devil Hills Lifesaving Station up in Corolla. It must have had some journey to get there, and it did. But there is more to the building than just that.

Built in 1878, it was one of several lifesaving stations built along the coast to help serve the ships that passed and occasionally became shipwrecks on the Outer Banks coast. Staffed by volunteers, the crew of the lifesaving station would await a call to row out and save the lives of those stranded in a storm as their ship floundered in the high seas. With the preponderance of ships in distress, the crews were never idle as much as they wished. But not all their adventure was on the sea. Some was in the air.

This station originally sat in Kill Devil Hills, on the beach just across from the Wright Brothers Memorial. Since it was built in 1878, it was actually there before the monument was built, and was also there when the Wrights first flew. The brothers were a curious sight to the surfmen, and they found a way to visit the inventors whenever the surf crew was off duty, taking mail or hauling firewood over. The lifesaving crew became so important to the Wrights that the brothers ultimately put up a red flag on a pole when they needed help assembling or moving their airplane. John T. Daniels, W.S. Dough, and Adam D. Etheridge were the surfmen on hand when Orville flew the first successful flight on December 17, 1903. Daniels even snapped the famous photo of the craft lifting up off its rail. Daniels would also get a humorous claim to fame, as he was caught up in the flyer when holding the craft down during a big gust of wind. The plane tumbled down the sand, with Daniels trapped in the wires. Unharmed except for a few bumps, he was able to claim to be both the pilot of the fifth flight at Kill Devil Hills, as well as the first airplane crash casualty.

The surfmen weren't the only important players in the Wright brothers story. The building itself played an important part in the first flights. After their success on December 17, the Wrights telegraphed their father to let them know of the accomplishments they made from the telegraph machine at the lifesaving station.

The station stayed in use until 1933. After that, the building fell into disrepair, being used as employee housing. Doug Twiddy of Twiddy Real Estate bought the building in order to restore it in 1986. It was cut into three pieces, separating the first and second story, as well as removing a storage wing. Placed on trucks, each piece was moved over 20 miles north to be placed in Corolla. The building was then restored, stitched together, and during that time, many discoveries were found. The original sign was found inside the building and restored, as well as an oar from one of the station's life boats, and even a hand written documentation of the wreck of a ship, the *Josephine*.

Now the building is restored to all its beauty. It is used as an office for Twiddy Real Estate, and displays much of the memorabilia found in the restoration, as well as collections of Wright Brothers items.

Corolla Ponies

36.37892° -75.83203°

The first visitors to Corolla were not the northern hunters to come down in the winter to shoot geese on the Atlantic Flyway. They were the wild Spanish mustangs that still wander the beaches and hills of Corolla to the Virginia line. No one is sure how the horses came to the area. They are very likely descendants of Spanish horses brought to the New World, though exactly how they got there is unknown. They may have been left behind by Spanish explorer Lucas Vasquez de Allyôn. The Spanish nobleman tried without success to create a Spanish settlement on the Atlantic coast. When attacked by the aboriginal tribes and run out, the settlers may have abandoned their horses to the area. Or the ponies could be descendants of Sir Richard Grenville's expedition, where one of his ships cracked up on the shore, releasing much of his animal supplies that he acquired in the West Indies onto the Outer Banks shores. This is likely how the Okracoke ponies came to be, and the Corolla horses could have a similar genetic source.

However they got there, they flourished for a very long time. It took until the 1980s for the horses to take a downward spiral. With development rampant and cars everywhere, horses were getting hit and killed as they wandered what used to be their empty beaches. It didn't help that new home owners put out such delicious plants to eat in their front yards. Between 1985 and 1996, twenty horses were hit by cars, injuring or killing the animals.

Due to the increasing danger to the horses, the Corolla Wild Horse Fund was formed, and two sound to sea fences were put up along the northern part of Currituck's Outer Banks. Installed in a mixture of private and public land, the few remaining horses were rounded up to be moved to a safer location. Today, the horses run free on both empty land and the newly developed homesites of Carova. The horses can be spotted in the dunes as well as playing on the beaches in the sand and surf.

Wild horses can be beautiful to see, as they are majestic and powerful animals. But they are also feral, large and dangerous. Because of that, and the risk of injury to the horse as well as human, people are instructed to always stay 50 feet away from a wild horse. Never approach or attempt to feed or pet a horse. While some may be docile and accustomed to human interaction, the Corolla horses need to remain wild creatures. If a horse approaches a person, it is the human's job to get away from the horse, no matter how fun it might be to see one up close. Failure to do so will result in some stiff penalties, and probably quite a bit of shaming by everyone else who knows better.

But there still are easy ways to see the horses. Several off road tours are offered by companies in Corolla, where visitors get to pile into an off-road vehicle and drive northward on

the beach. Sitting in the open air comfort of a big truck led by a guide who does all the driving is much better than going out on your own and getting stuck. And there is much more to see than just the beach and ponies.

The best way to learn about the Corolla horses is to visit the Corolla Horse Fund Museum. There visitors can see pictures of the horses, learn about the conservation efforts, and even have a chance to see some of the horses that are used for instruction or are in rehabilitation.

Penny's Hill

36.42825° -75.84015°

Penny's Hill has long been the destination of off roaders, four wheel drive vehicles, and just anyone who wants to play in the big sand dune north of Corolla. The big hill is the second largest dune in North Carolina, rivaled only by Jockey's Ridge to the south. Penny's Hill differs in other ways to its more famous cousin to the south. Penny's Hill is accessible by four wheel drive, and has been used as a spot for sand rails, dune buggies, and trucks for years.

Penny's Hill has some unique history to it. It used to be part of a small chain of dunes, which included Lewark's Hill. Lewark's Hill sat next to the small town of Seagull. Right up until it sat on top of the town. The dune slowly moved its way over the little village, covering and filling the buildings with sand. Lewark's Hill finally took the little town sometime in the 1950s. Penny's Hill had separated from the dune and had migrated north, past the New Currituck Inlet, a waterway that was cut through the land and had in the past allowed ships access to the sound from the Atlantic. By the time the Ash

Wednesday Storm blew through the coast, it took part of Penny's Hill with it, filling in the inlet with half of the dune. This is partly what created Penny's Hill's bowl shape.

Today Lewark's Hill is mostly hidden, covered by growth, but still moving. As much as it moved over the town, it now has started to move past the town, and parts are being uncovered. A cemetery and a bit of chimney now peek through the sand. Finding them is difficult. The area is natural, with all that comes to it. Plants, briars, pokey twigs are the least of any explorer's worry. There are also wild animals out there. Exploring is at your own risk.

Penny's Hill is more accessible, but the only way to get there is by four wheel drive. It's a great place to pull up and picnic.

Wash Woods Station

36.49945° -75.85955°

Wash Woods Coast Guard Station was named after a small village that, oddly or appropriately, was formed from a shipwreck. The town of Wash Woods was formed sometime between 1889 and 1895 from the survivors of a shipwreck off the southern Virginia coast. The residents built homes, churches and stores with the wood from shipwrecks that washed up. Wash Woods Station was built in 1917 as a replacement for an outmoded station farther north.

The station served as a home to coastguardsmen who performed several rescues along the barren north coast of North Carolina. During World War II, it was home to about 30 guardsmen who kept a lookout for both German U-Boats and any infiltrators who may foolishly try to slip into the islands to cause damage. After the war, with advances in safety, the number of guardsmen went down, until only a caretaker remained, before being closed around 1955.

During the 1970s, growth began in nearby Corolla, and Carova started to see the occasional visit by off road vehicle. The station served as a vacation house until 1988, when it was sold to the Twiddy family, who had done the restoration of the Kill Devil Hills station. The Twiddys restored the main building, with 8 bedrooms and two baths, the cisterns that were used to collect rainwater off the roof for the guardsmen, as well as an observation tower. After an extensive restoration, where paneling and carpet were removed to find the original walls and floor underneath, the building was used as a real estate office and later as a rental unit for people who wanted to experience a more traditional stay on the coast. The Twiddys even rebuilt the observation tower to the original plans of the station.

The building is open for visits, with interesting decorations and photos on the walls, as it is still used as a rental office. But to get there, visitors are going to need four wheel drive, and the skill to drive the sands of Carova. Driving on the beach is not for the unskilled, and it takes more than just all-wheel drive to get up there. Take the good advice from experts first, or maybe just catch a ride with someone else.

Dog Track Speedway

Moyock   36.54608° -76.19159°

Greyhound racing became a highly popular spectator sport after 1919, when the first oval track was opened in California. By the 1930s, tracks with a mechanical hare to chase had opened all over the country. The sport was popular with working class men, as they could go to the tracks after work and gamble on the races. But due to the gambling, and the unsavory activities that often go with that, some tracks and clubs were shut down over time.

In the 1930s, the Cavalier Kennel Club of Norfolk, Virginia, was shut down, and the owners moved just south of the North Carolina border into Moyock. There they built a quarter mile track to host dog races. Free from the focus of anti-gambling groups in Virginia, but close enough to attract naval servicemen to cross the border and bet on the race, the track flourished for a time. Dog races were especially popular after World War II with people in the Hampton Roads area. It wouldn't be until 1954 when the NC legislature upheld an anti dog racing law that the track would be shut down.

But that alone didn't stop the track. In September of 1962, the track was reopened as a quarter mile race track for NASCAR. Ned Jarrett won the pole and the race, and went on to become the track's most successful driver, with 4 wins out of its seven events from 1962 through 1966. With bigger tracks and better purses to be won, the track fell by the wayside when NASCAR became more successful.

For a time in the 1970s, the track was almost lost to development. The track land was bought with the intention of the property being redeveloped into retirement homes. Workers came in to demolish the track, but it proved an unyielding task.

The track was no longer used, but still visible from the road. Especially noticeable were the lights for the parking lots and the tall grandstands. Sadly, the wooden stands, already rickety from being unused and in disrepair, burned to the ground one night. The blaze lit up the night sky, and by morning there was nothing left but smoking cinders.

Today the track is being reclaimed by the natural land around it. The path that the cars, and dogs, took is still visible, but it is mostly a muddy bog, home to more mosquitoes than machines. The concrete slab that the grandstands sat upon still exists, as do the light poles for the parking lot.

Oddity ★

Racing, whether dog or car or horse, was a popular pastime in towns big and small, as long as they could carve out a big enough circle in a field somewhere, and at least two people thought they were the fastest around.

Difficulty ★★

Most of the track has succumbed to nature by now, but the remains of the parking lot and lights are still there. The old stands were a recognizable sight before they burned down.

Edenton Tea Pot

Edenton 36.05715° -76.60833°

It may be surprising to know that hundreds of years ago news still traveled fast, bad news even more so. While the southern states with their agricultural production were largely immune to the greater impact of British rule and taxation, the people of North Carolina saw themselves more aligned with the people of Massachusetts than with a parliament thousands of miles away separated by an entire ocean. So, when the people of New England were continually punished by unfair acts meant to raise money for Britain without any representation, and then followed up with the Coercive Acts, which effectively stripped the elective government from Massachusetts, the people of North Carolina felt compelled to act.

The first action came from the First Provincial Congress in New Bern, where 71 representatives from the North Carolina counties met to express support for a Continental Congress, which later met in Philadelphia. In addition, the First Provincial Congress also called for a boycott of British goods into the colonies. Boycotts had been used before, and the Continental Congress would later call for a boycott of British goods in hopes to punish Britain without resorting to war, though even then most leaders saw armed conflict the only likely scenario.

The North Carolina Provincial Congress's call to boycott British trade quickly made its way to Edenton. A group of 51 women in Edenton, led by Penelope Barker and Elizabeth King, pledged in writing to no longer purchase English tea leaves or English cloth. This was an important act in many ways. It was the first act of political resistance to the overarching and punishing acts that Britain enacted on New England, done by a group of women. Giving up tea was a decidedly dramatic event, as it was consumed regularly, and its use was symbolic of social standing. In England the letter had a polarizing effect. Opposition by a group of women was unheard of, and the news was rather surprising to the English. However, a letter sent by women was not taken seriously by some, as men in England did not fear the boycott being done by a group of females. But in the colonies, it really made waves. The Edenton Tea Party showed that the colonies were fairly united in the protest of the actions that England was doing in Boston. It showed an act of patriotism and unity across borders, cultures, and regions.

To commemorate the event, and its repercussions, an emblem of the party was installed in the courthouse green. A teapot is displayed on the top of a cannon, upended and placed in the ground. In 1905, Baldwin Brass Company of Bridgeport, Connecticut, cast the teapot in their foundry. Mr. Baldwin himself had recently visited Edenton to see the location of the battle of the Albemarle from the Civil War. He found himself so well treated and welcomed that he made the teapot and sent it as a note of thanks. In addition to the teapot, other cannons grace the area. The big guns were purchased by Benjamin Franklin in France to help secure the defense of Edenton harbor. The Chowan County Courthouse was built in 1767, and is considered the most original colonial courthouse in America.

Now Edenton is a quiet town, great for walks through the old neighborhoods, visits to the local restaurants, and even stopping for a cup of tea. Not only can travelers see the spot of one of the first boycotts against British rule in the colonies, they can also have a spot of tea while doing it.

Oddity ★★

It's a popular little sight to see. It's attached to a cannon, so you can't pour from it. Which probably is appropriate, since the town was boycotting all things British. This teapot shouldn't have any tea in it, right?

Difficulty ★

Since it is fairly small, seeing it means getting out of the car. Also, the park is on a narrow road, so it probably is better to park on the waterfront and walk over. This is a great place for walking, anyway, so if you are walking over, you are doing it right.

Penelope Barker definitely made a splash with her boycott of British goods, but it didn't help her husband much. John Barker was the North Carolina representative to the English Parliament. He had to escape London to France, and did not return to North Carolina until 1778.

Fossil Pit

Aurora   35.30445° -76.78737°

Hidden under all the recent history of North Carolina is a truly ancient land. In a state where going back only to the 1970s would find a change from a farm society to a growth of big business, or looking back at old black and white photos of the turn of the last century would find clean windswept beaches where the first airplane took off, or even over 400 years ago when the natives of this land first saw European settlers stepping ashore, it is difficult to picture the coast of the state at over 250 million years ago.

At that time, North Carolina, and all of North America, was joined to Africa in a supercontinent called Pangea. As what would become the Atlantic Ocean slowly spread out, the top part of the coastal plain of North Carolina ripped off the rest of the land and went with Africa. This is why today the coastal lands are low and poorly drained compared to the rocky Piedmont. It also left a low spot where the growing ocean could fill in. The northeast coastal land became filled with a deep sediment, along with a large amount of sea life, over millions of years, as the sea level rose and ebbed along the coast.

Around 5 million years ago, the area around Aurora was deeply inundated, and actually was part of a deep sea. At this time the waters were ruled by giant ancient whales and the dreaded megalodon, a prehistoric forerunner to today's sharks. It would take millions of years for the sea level to lower, rise, lower, myriad times, until it reached the fairly recognizable slope of today.

And today it is actually pretty easy to see all these histories in the filmy sands of the coast, going back all those millions of years. The Potash Corporation runs a phosphate open mine at Aurora, where they strip off the upper layers of sediment to get to phosphate rich soils. Digging down about 15 million years only goes about 120 to 170 feet below the surface. Most of the land is stripped off to get to the phosphate soils at this depth. While the Potash Corporation is interested in getting to the phosphate below all the overburden soil, all the other good stuff is in the soil on top.

The upper layer shows all the creatures from the recent past, a mere tick of the clock in geologic time. The upper level has various fossils appearing near the surface, including preserved giant trees, as well as large mammal teeth. Most notably from this period would be the preserved tusks of ancient mastodon which roamed the swampy marshes of North Carolina thousands of years ago. Also found were the teeth of early horses which called the region home.

Digging deeper found other prizes. The earlier times of the land being submerged meant that sea life remains are abundant in the stripped upper soils. Not only can sea shell fossils be found, including whole giant scallops, more prized are the teeth of the megalodon. The giant teeth are discovered there regularly. A megalodon tooth will appear large and black, easily the size of a person's hand, intimating a jaw big enough to bite a modern great white in half. The shark, technically named *Carcharodon* megalodon, truly must have been a beast of the seas. At 50 feet long and weighing in at up to 50 tons, it feasted on whales, as evidence of the shark's bite on whale bones that has been found. Megalodon roamed the oceans as a truly cosmopolitan hunter, its remains found all over the world. It must have found ancient North

Carolina particularly agreeable, as its teeth are found here in abundance.

With all the fossilized treasures being churned up at the phosphate pit, fossil hunters came in hoards to visit the site. For a time it was possible to sort through the spoil beds, looking for shark teeth and other fossils. But the open mine no longer allows visitors or offers tours.

Fortunately, they found another use for all that extra soil. Now visitors to Aurora's downtown fossil museum can dig through giant piles of soil to find hidden fossils, sharks' teeth, shells, and other ancient rewards. Shark's teeth are a common find, and the prized giant tooth of the Megalodon can be found on occasion. Two or three a month are found in the pit. The museum itself is a reward to visitors. There is a very large collection of sharks' teeth on display, numerous examples of different sharks' choppers that were found at the nearby mine. There are also whale and stingray fossils in the museum.

Oddity ★★

The museum is a nice visit for kids especially, but adults will learn a lot, too. Dinosaurs abound at the big museums, but finding a nice little place like this is cool in that it shows off the mammal and marine life that lived on the North Carolina coast long ago.

Difficulty ★★

The museum is right in the middle of downtown Aurora, and is easy to find. But to dig in the Pits of the Pungo, you may want to bring a bucket and trowel for your kids, maybe gloves, change of clothes... shark repellant.

Pepsi Birthplace

New Bern   35.10670° -77.03975°

New Bern was founded in 1710 making it the second oldest town in North Carolina. The town became the first capitol of the state, and the population grew in the little city on the Neuse River. With a warm summer climate, the people probably grew thirsty for a cool drink in town. Too bad they had to wait almost 200 years until they got one.

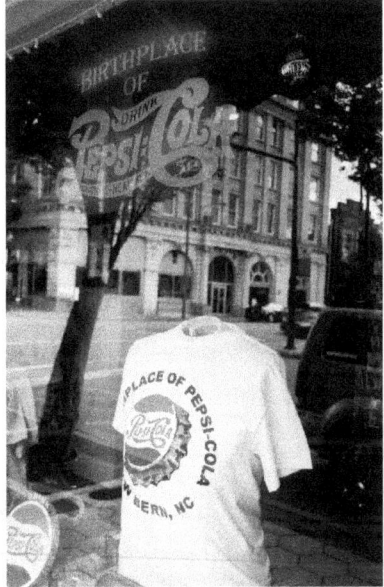

Pepsi was created by Caleb Davis Bradham in 1893. He had moved to New Bern where he opened a pharmacy and mixed together a concoction of water, sugar, caramel, lemon oil and nutmeg, to create a soda he named after himself. Calling it "Brad's Drink," it was meant more to help with digestion, fighting dyspepsia, or indigestion. The drink's name soon took the name Pepsi, from the symptoms it was fighting. The soda was an instant hit in the town, and by 1902 the Pepsi-Cola company was formed.

Sales were great for the drink, with almost 20,000 gallons of the syrup base being sold. Franchises were sold, and the drink started going into bottles. By 1910 the drink could be found in 24 states. Pepsi stayed popular for years until the beginning of World War I. Severe rationing of sugar at the time, as well as a high cost for the sweetener, meant that Bradham couldn't afford enough sugar to meet demand of his customers. He was further impacted when after the war, sugar costs skyrocketed as price controls were removed by the government. In order to fill his supply, Bradham bought a huge amount of sugar, which sent his company into a downward spiral. Though still popular, people expected the drink to cost 5 cents. Pepsi couldn't cover the cost of making the drink, and the company went bankrupt.

With its assets sold to the president of a candy company, Pepsi moved out of North Carolina. While the company, and the drink, thrived, it no longer had a presence in New Bern. Bradham returned to his pharmacy, as he still in his heart cared for the health of people, same as when he invented the drink years before. He even continued a scholarship for pharmacy students at UNC up until 1930. He passed away in 1934, and is interred in New Bern.

Pepsi the company may be gone, but Pepsi the product is still front and center in New Bern. The original pharmacy has been turned into a mixture of old time soda fountain, gift shop, and museum. Visitors can come in any day and have a Pepsi. Then spend time looking at the old memorabilia. There is a large collection of old Pepsi bottles, old signs, and great displays. The gift shop offers plenty of Pepsi items for sale for fans of the drink, from clothes to glasses to key chains. And not only Pepsi, but there are several things for sale for Mountain Dew fans, too. The fountain even offers a new version of Brad's Drink, called Caleb's Kola, a nod to the new trend of craft sodas, made with natural ingredients and spices.

Oddity ★

The museum is a great little bit of history in a very historical town. Great place to stop if you are thirsty, too.

Difficulty ★

The Pepsi museum is open every day in downtown New Bern. The only issue you may have is parking on the street. Oh, and don't order a Coke anywhere.

In 1906 the federal government passed the Pure Food and Drug Act, which banned toxic substances such as uranium, lead, and arsenic from foods and drinks. Yes, there actually had to be a law for this. Most drinks had to change their recipes, but Pepsi was already free of any banned substances.

Cheerwine was also invented in North Carolina. The cherry soda was dreamed up in Salisbury.

Voice of America

Greenville   35.69777° -77.15422°

In the early days of World War II, even before the United States entered into fighting after the attack on Pearl Harbor, the U.S. began shortwave radio broadcasts to counter Nazi propaganda that was being spread through Latin and South America. After entering the war, the U.S. created a live radio broadcast in shortwave that first transmitted from New York City on February 1, 1942. Called *Voices from America*, it broadcast news of the war in German to the people in Germany at the beginning of the war. It became known as The Voice of America, the network that would broadcast information and pro U.S. policy across two oceans through Europe, the Middle East, and the Pacific.

Soon after the war ended, most broadcasting ended as well, but in 1947 programming resumed with news and music directed not only at the newly peaceful Europe, but also to the Soviet Union and Soviet bloc countries in Eastern Europe in order to counter the misinformation that the USSR began spreading in their controlled countries. In order to keep broadcasting the U.S. national message, new towers and centers needed to be built. The transmitters in New York and New Jersey were continually becoming more outdated, and a new place was selected in the 1950s. A rural and empty area near Greenville was selected, and after years of setbacks, the Voice of America station was finally begun in 1960, with the broadcast finally going live in 1963 after a dedication by President John F. Kennedy.

The site originally consisted of three different locations, serving different areas of the globe with their powerful antennas. The three sites became the largest and most powerful broadcast sites in the world, with each having multiple transmitters cranking out a total of 2.4 million watts at each location. Over the years, the shortwave broadcasters have sent news and music to nearly every place on earth. With changes in world politics, the message of Voice of America also changed over time. Focus shifted from Europe and Russia after the fall of the Soviet Union, and other locations got more attention, especially in the Middle East. When Haiti experienced a massive earthquake in 2010, the VOA changed its broadcasting in the island language from 2 hours to 15 hours a day.

Today, while the VOA still exists, much of the sites around Greenville are no longer used. VOA broadcasts in many places locally, or through the internet. Site B still broadcasts its news and music format 24 hours a day across the world, but the other sites are now being used for other purposes. Site A may be returned to a natural setting, as it has not been used since 2006, except as a nesting site for birds. The most active spot is Site C, home of the Edward R. Murrow Transmitting Station. The building still has its somewhat Cold War era look, and a large satellite dish still sits out front, guarded by a closed and disused pillbox-like guardhouse. The building now has a new and unique purpose. The building was sold to East Carolina University in

2001, and is being used as a storage and curation area for the artifacts being brought up from Blackbeard's ship, *Queen Anne's Revenge*.

Oddity ★

The open fields and huge array of antennas is somewhat striking and mysterious, with an old Cold War vibe still in the air. Visitors will wonder who is watching them, some black trench coat figure, taking pictures surreptitiously with a tiny camera, and sending it back to a clandestine spy lab up in D.C.

Difficulty ★

The location has always been known as the Voice of America, though now with it being closed from its original purpose, getting to the old buildings is a little easier. They are a little out in the middle of nowhere. The Murrow Building is not usually open to visitors, but short wave radio groups have arranged tours to see the massive gear used inside.

Looking To The Sky

A Did You See That? Detour

North Carolina has long been famous for its place in a moment back in December of 1903, when the Wright Brothers were able to launch their plane into the air, creating the first successful and viable airplane. Their accomplishment has been noted as one of the most important inventions of all time. The iconic photo of Orville flying off the rail in the sands near Kill Devil Hill while Wilbur stares on in amazement was the first time an invention was ever captured on a photograph at the moment of accomplishment. So singular an achievement it was that North Carolina placed the airplane on their license plates with the slogan "First In Flight."

But North Carolina has been the location of more than one rather important aerial achievement. As a matter of fact, the Tar Heel State has seen just about every type of aircraft that has been flown, or attempted to be flown, from its lands. Not all of the places have spots to visit, but the history is certainly spectacular. So keep watching the skies...

Gatling Airplane

Murfreesboro   36.44309° -77.09700°

Henry Gatling, brother of Gatling Gun inventor Richard, was born in Hertford County. Between 1872 and 1873, he built a flying machine meant to mimic the flight of buzzards, with hand cranked blowers and moveable wings. It "flew" once, in 1873, from a raised platform down a hill for about 100 feet, until it crashed and was irreparably damaged. Some observers say it did not so much fly as glide, while later historians believe that the description of the flight even in that way may have been too kind, and that the plane simply crashed. It was destroyed in a barn fire in 1905.

Enthusiasts have gathered information from photos and documents to create a replica at the Murfreesboro Transportation Museum. It is available for viewing upon request during the week at business hours. The town requests that visitors call ahead (252-398-5922) to allow time to get someone to unlock the museum.

Bumblebee Helicopter

Beaufort   34.71755° -76.66650°

William Luther Paul may not have had much formal education, having left school after finishing only the seventh grade, but that didn't stop him from having a serious mechanical curiosity. He designed and built an early helicopter which he named the Bumblebee. It was similar in some ways to both a modern Shinook helicopter, with two sets of blades, as well as like a gyrocopter, with a propeller on the back to push the craft along. In 1907, the craft actually flew, lifting off the ground of Paul's hangar and hovering five feet off the ground. It wouldn't yet hold his weight, but he was on the right track. His biggest setback was actually caused by someone else. In 1908, Orville Wright crashed one of his planes, killing the passenger. Paul's wife was so terrified that she begged him to stop. He didn't work on it again until 1942, when he sent his plans to the Department of Commerce, who sadly rejected his ideas.

A replica of his helicopter is at the Maritime Museum in Beaufort, but may not be on display.

Blimp Hangar

Weeksville   36.22923° -76.135313°

The world's largest wooden structure, an enormous blimp hangar, used to exist at the Weeksville naval air station, a lighter than air blimp facility built to help in the patrol of the Atlantic coast. Another structure still sits on the land, a hangar for blimps and aerostats for Tethered Communications of Maryland, who build blimps and tethered balloons. Tours can be arranged in advance. Read more about the base and its history in *Did You See That? A GPS Guide to North Carolina's Out of the Ordinary Attractions.*

Operation Bumblebee

Topsail Beach   34.36723° -77.62968°

Operation Bumblebee was an early attempt by the U.S. Navy to test ramjet technology in rockets. The then empty beach and open sea were good locations to shoot off missiles into the water. But with increased fishing boat traffic, the location was shut down and ultimately ended up at White Sands Missile Range. Today, there are several of the original spotting towers still visible, some converted into homes, and the assembly building is now the Missiles and More Museum. The launching pad was where the Jolly Roger Inn is now. Read more about Operation Bumblebee, and learn of some of the tower locations, in *Did You See That? A GPS Guide to North Carolina's Out of the Ordinary Attractions.*

Other Wright Monument

Kitty Hawk   36.06219° -75.70111°

   While it is often attributed that the Wrights first flew in Kitty Hawk, it is more accurate to say they flew in what is now Kill Devil Hills, in an open and windy stretch of land near Big Kill Devil Hill. But they did actually first stay in Kitty Hawk, camping in the dunes near Kitty Hawk Village, and building their first glider there. The residents of Kitty Hawk put up a small obelisk in front of the Tate family home where the Wrights stayed on their early trips. The marker was removed to the town hall after it was damaged, and a replacement was placed in the same spot. Read more about the Wright Brothers Monument in *Did You See That? On The Outer Banks*.

Central

Coats Bell Collection

Angier 35.50883° -78.60512°

Visitors to the bell collection on the land once owned by Robert "Tink" Coats and his wife Addie might wonder why someone would collect large bells like Tink did. Bells would seem to be such an anomalous choice for collecting. They are heavy, cumbersome, difficult to mount, and hardly necessary any more. Yet to Tink, he saw a value in them. Enough that when someone had one for sale, he went out in search of the bell, and then brought it back home.

There could be a good reason for Coats's love of bells. He was a principal, and his wife was a teacher, so there may have been some natural attraction to school bells. And when they moved from Elizabeth City to the McGee's Crossroads area of Angier, the couple helped to create fire departments and worked to get paved roads across the towns, so Tink may have also had a bit of an attraction to old fire bells. But no one really knows why he collected them.

The collection actually consists of several different types of bells. There are the school bells and fire bells, but there are also bells from churches and trains. In 1969, when Tink knew he was getting too old to do much with them, he commissioned a tower to hang all his bells. He wanted to get the bells up and able to ring, as well as leave them displayed so that his wife didn't have to worry about the bells when he passed. Fortunately, Tink lived until 1972 and got to see the fruits of his work, with 32 bells displayed on a grand rig of metal, a steel tower of sound, with the bells hung so that ropes could be pulled to ring them all. Tink rang them on a regular schedule. Every Sunday at 9 am, he rang the bells. Other than that, the bells were only rung on Easter, July 4, and New Year's Eve. Of course, if someone wanted to hear the bells, they could be rung by someone else.

Today, the bells are mostly silent. The land was donated to the Pleasant Grove Homemakers Club, and consists of not only the bell collection, but also the Coats Museum, which holds a collection of old farm equipment, as well as Addie Coats's 1953 Cadillac. The museum is only open the second Wednesday of every month. They have the ability to pay staff to be open every day, but the rural location makes visitors a rare appearance. The museum is also open by appointment. The bells outside can be seen, and rung, at any time. Locals still gather on July 4 to ring the bells, just as Tink Coats did.

Oddity ★★★

Travelers may take a day off from school to go on an adventure into Angier and McGee's Crossroads to see the Coats Museum and school bell collection. A day off is sometimes needed. But don't let those school bells send anyone back to class!

Difficulty ★

The Coats Museum is only open one day a month, but people can still go by any time to see the bell collection. The Coats homestead has an address in Angier, but it is closer to McGee's Crossroads. Angier has several festivals, including the Crepe Myrtle Festival, and a summertime motorcycle event.

Gourd Museum

Angier 35.50758° -78.74052°

If it wasn't strange enough to have someone collect bells in the town of Angier, there was also a gourd collector, too. Actually, it may not be that surprising. Gourd growing and collecting is a popular pastime in North Carolina. The NC Gourd Society is so popular that it not only meets at the Gourd Museum, the members also have a satellite gourd patch in the western part of the state so that hobbyists don't have to drive all the way to Angier from the mountains. And the society also has Gourd Days at the Raleigh Farmer's Market, selling seeds and memorabilia.

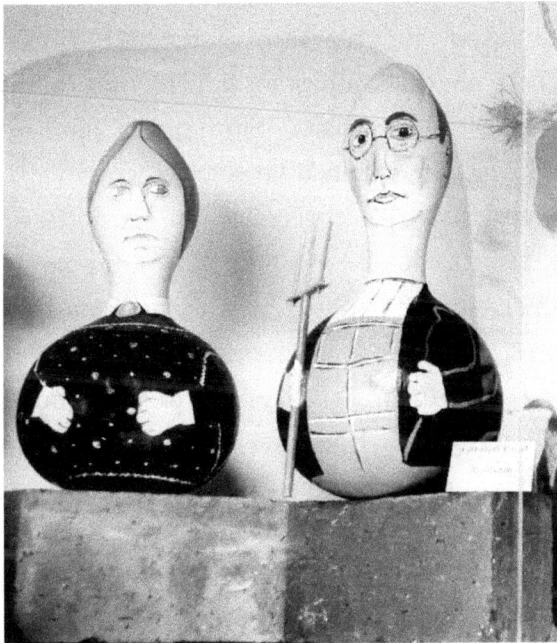

Marvin Johnson became interested in gourds after remembering how his mother would grow them, getting his brothers and him to tuck the gourds under the warm tin roof to dry them. He started growing gourds, the usual ones that are used for decorations, and later growing larger and more unique types. He grew large gourds, used as dippers for water and bushel basket gourds that could be dried, carved, and used to hold or carry things. They are so strong that Johnson would often be photographed standing on one.

Johnson grew more than 200 different kinds of gourds, and collected many others from around the world. He was rewarded with numerous blue ribbons from the NC state fair, as well as a collection so big it started overwhelming the house, and his wife Mary. In 1964 Marvin moved his collection to a new building he built, and the Marvin Johnson Gourd Museum was created.

The collection grew as the Johnsons gathered more and more gourds, some used for practical purposes, others made into decorations. There are dolls and other figures, musical instruments like xylophones and drums, baskets, birdhouses, and even the light fixtures. All this was housed in a little white shed with green doors. Marvin and Mary cared for the collection, open free of charge to anyone, until Mary's death and Marvin's retirement. He left the property in the care of his nephew. When Marvin passed away in 2003, the property was left to the local church. When the Johnson farm was sold, the church and town got together to make sure the amazing collection was kept together and available to view. Marvin Johnson's gourd collection was moved to the Angier Municipal Building, where it is available for viewing 5 days a week.

Oddity ★

The passion that Marvin Johnson must have had is evident in the vastness of this collection. It may seem like something simple, but this historical compilation is now a famous NC roadside attraction. There just aren't collections like this everywhere.

Difficulty ★

As long as you go during banking hours, you should be okay to see this.

Giants Among Us

A Did You See That? Detour

They tower over us, these men and women. Giants who compete with the Long Leaf Pine for dominance in the Carolina Blue skies. Yes, there still are giants on the earth these days, though they seem to stay where they are rather than walk across the state. Muffler Men, Pioneer Giants, Uniroyal Gals, and Giant Indians grace many parts of the state. They are, and were for a long time, icons of advertising.

The fiberglass figures were first created in 1962 by Bob Prewitt in Venice, CA. He had been making fiberglass animal statues, prancing horses and the like, for a while, and someone called to order a 20 foot tall Paul Bunyan statue. Prewitt made the statue in one piece, but the buyer fell through. So Prewitt put the statue on a truck and went driving to find a buyer on Route 66. He knew he found the right place at Flagstaff, AZ, when he pulled up to the Lumberjack Café. Soon, an industry was formed.

Steve Dashew, a boatbuilder, had bought Prewitt's business, and renamed it International Fiberglass. He acquired much of Prewitt's tools, including some of the animal molds and the Paul Bunyan mold. He figured that the casts would be a good side business for when he wasn't making boats. Considering the popularity of the giants that would come, he was right. The second Paul Bunyan figure was cast in four pieces for easier transport and assembled at the location. Soon, the individual parts could be customized for the purchaser. Heads and arms could be made separate, in different poses. Which meant that cowboys were able to be made for Phillips 66 gas stations, Giant Indians for Pontiac dealers, and Vikings for Viking Carpets. In addition, International Fiberglass made a completely unique figure called the

Uniroyal Gal, for Uniroyal Tires. She was special in that she could dress, or undress, for the occasion. Normally sporting a shirt and miniskirt, the fiberglass clothes could be removed to show off her bikini underneath.

An even more rare and unique fiberglass figure is the Pioneer Giant. Originally it was made as a decoration for the Wagon Ho! restaurant chain. The original figure sat on the awning of the restaurant, one arm up, and one across. The restaurant itself was built like a giant wagon, complete with cloth top, and the figure was meant to hold the reins to a team of imaginary horses and a whip, but it is unlikely he ever did. The restaurant chain failed, and of the few figures ever made by International Fiberglass, only two still exist.

But that didn't keep a good Pioneer Giant down. Later, it seems that Unique Fiberglass Figures out of Rocky Mount either acquired a mold of the Pioneer Giant, or made one. They began making a standing version of the figure, but with the same hand position. There are at least 6 standing Pioneer Giants in existence, and 5 of those reside somewhere in North Carolina.

With the growing popularity of the figures, it is no surprise that more are being made. After creating a simple mold, the lightweight figures are easily cast out of fiberglass. They are big, but relatively easy to install, and repair. Due to this, another fiberglass company in NC has been making the figures. Graham & Dolce Fiberglass now have a serious menagerie of fiberglass animals and Uniroyal Gals on their property.

And more figures keep coming. So if you see a giant pirate, or a beach babe, she may have been made right here in North Carolina. Or they could have come a long way, from another beach, far on the west coast. Either way, whatever trip they took makes it worthwhile to take a trip around the state to find them here. This is not an inclusive list, as new figures seem to be popping up all the time, but it's a start.

Otway Pirate

Otway 34.77740° -76.55972°

Not a muffler man, but a custom made pirate to honor, well, pirates. It is sometimes referred to as a Blackbeard statue, but Otway Burns also made his way around the area for a while. It doesn't look like either one. It looks like a pirate. It's next to a marine repair and sales shop in Otway, near Beaufort.

Paul Bunyan and Babe the Blue Ox

Rocky Mount 36.06012° -77.82609°

An original International Fiberglass figure of Paul Bunyan. Can be seen from the interstate. So be careful while driving.

Muffler Men

Wilson 35.71808° -77.92076°

35.71679° -77.90582°

White's Tire Service in Wilson has two good looking muffler men. Actually they are tire men. Both hold tires, and one is on the roof of a store.

Bradsher Landscape Muffler Man

Raleigh   35.88056° -78.57813°

He's well cared for in Bradsher Landscape's parking lot.

Puncheon Camp Creek Ranch Muffler Man

Edneyville   35.41968° -82.37291°

Mostly hidden on a private old west ranch, if you look closely from the road you can see a Muffler Man. There are some other big statues on the ranch as well, including a Giant Indian and some giant cows.

Antique Pioneer Giant

Hillsborough   36.05823° -79.10295°

Pioneering great prices at Hillsborough's antique mall for years.

Bill The Pioneer Giant

Linwood   35.75611° -80.34584°

Welcome to...
The Shops at
Daniel Boone

A truckstop staple for years on Highway 70, but he can only be accessed by the frontage road.

Pioneer Giant Shriner

Roanoke Rapids   36.39294° -77.63141°

Read more about this guy in *Did You See That? A GPS Guide to North Carolina's Out of the Ordinary Attractions.*

Pioneer Pirate

Kill Devil Hills   36.03398° -75.68312°

It's hidden in the backyard, but a little bit might be visible. Don't go snooping, or his pirate pals might make you walk the plank. He used to be in front of the old Forbes Mini Golf.

Chief Willy

Asheville   35.61844° -82.62639°

Chief Willy is the mascot for the Erwin High School Chiefs. It is close to the school, next to the parking lot for students. Visiting this one would be best done during a football game or when school is out, so as not to look creepy while walking around a high school when class is in session.

Chief Pontiac

Asheville   35.58840° -82.58900°

Harry's on the Hill is a General Motors dealership that, before the make went under, sold Pontiacs as well as Buicks and Caddys. Chief Pontiac stands inside the lot, between Harry's and the other businesses on Patton Ave.

Tattoo Parlor Indian

Cherokee   35.46852° -83.29575°

He's a little tattered, as his headdress has long been falling apart. But that may be appropriate, since the Cherokee never wore that stuff, anyway. He is noted for having haunting pale blue eyes.

Men's Night Out Uniroyal Gal

Rocky Mount   35.97443° -77.73763°

Not visible from the road unless the leaves are gone from the trees, and on private property of Men's Night Out, a private club, stands a Uniroyal Gal who used to be in front of Mosley's Shady Lake Motel.

Graham & Dolce Fiberglass

Bolton   34.31710° -78.24364°

They have several new figures of Uniroyal Gals, and they can make one for you. See them from the road.

Here's a couple curious facts about these giants. The term "Muffler Man" was actually coined by Roadside America. They noticed that many of the Paul Bunyan figures had been repurposed to advertise for car repair, and were holding mufflers. They weren't originally made for this purpose. And the Uniroyal Gal? Well, she was made for Uniroyal, but there was no exclusive license with International Fiberglass, so she was sold by them as Miss America, and any company could get one.

Hattadare Indian Reservation

Bunnlevel   35.33023° -78.78313°

The depiction of the Native American "Indian" of 1950s and 60s TV did little to accurately depict what the indigenous peoples of most parts of the U.S. looked like, especially the natives of North Carolina. Woodland Cherokee would have felt silly in the plains headdresses seen on shows like F Troop back in the 60s. And winters in the state would not go over well in just breechcloths.

Native American culture was on the mind of James Lowery when he created the Hattadare Indian Nation Park near Bunnlevel back in 1978. Lowery, a TV repairman with a bit of native blood in him, decided to build the park in order to have a place for the various tribes of eastern North Carolina to come together and unite and just hang out. Lowery believed that the tribes were all descendants of the Haterask (or current day Hatteras) Indians, as well as progeny of the original Lost Colony, including Virginia Dare and her family. Thus the name Hattadare.

Lowery's vision was probably less one of a roadside attraction, and more of a historical walking path and picnic area. The land near his trailer home was a clear and open path, due to the power lines running alongside the nearby highway. Lowery and his sons enlarged the land by clearing brush and trees to create a more open space. It was decorated with some concrete Indian figures and depictions of historical events, such as Virginia Dare's birth, and the meeting of Chief Manteo with the English colonists on Roanoke Island. Lowery built the statues in the park himself out of concrete and fiberglass. Lowery added little wooden shelters over the scenes to protect them from the elements. By the 1980s Lowery had included animals in the park, peacocks and ducks. With this much appeal, Lowery soon was leading school field trips full of kids through his not so little park to see his creation.

The central decoration in the park was the World's Largest Arrowhead, a large concrete obelisk dotted with small stones and a picture of Lowery himself in the middle. Lowery was given the nickname Chief Little Beaver due to a coon skin cap that he often wore. Lowery had some native DNA in him, though probably not Lumbee. However, he saw the various tribes of the east as having one central history. He theorized that all the later tribes came from the original English settlers and the coastal natives that lived along North Carolina's barrier islands. In 1968, he had written his Declaration of the Hattadare Nation, which put forth his theory. But more than that, he saw this idea as an ability for the various tribes to petition the government to gain federal recognition. While the unification of tribes, and the federal recognition, never came to fruition, it was the impetus to build the park.

Lowery passed away in 1990, and the park fell into disrepair for a time. Many of the statues had been overtaken by the plants and trees that Lowery and his children cleared years before. Hidden in the brush were bears and tiny cacti, the decorations placed years ago for the entertainment of visiting school kids. Storms and neglect took their toll on the park.

But the Hattadare Indian Nation has made a bit of a comeback in the past few years. Lowery's widow, Letha, wanted to see the park kept up, and encouraged their children to do so. While some had moved away, Charlie Lowery's son, Charlie, Jr., now cares for the area. The wooden covers have been repaired, and the land has been cleared again. Today people can still stop by and see the park, a tribute not only to the Lumbee and all the other tribes of eastern North Carolina, but to Charlie Lowery, Chief Little Beaver himself.

Oddity ★★★

There is not as much left as when it was new. The paint is fading on the statues, and there is less of a sense of wonder and more a sense of what was. But it still is a very strange thing, these statues and displays. That arrowhead is so abstract, not really like an arrowhead at all. There still resides a passion that Lowery had, hidden in the displays.

Difficulty ★★

Look for the big black fiberglass horse rearing up at the entrance, as well as the sign and a pyramid underneath it. Remember that while this place is open and meant for touring, there still are homes there, and you should be respectful as to where you park and how you act.

Chief Little Beaver is still in the park, in spirit and body, so to speak. Lowery was cremated and most of his ashes were scattered around the park. A small amount is buried in a little file box near the World's Largest Arrowhead at the end of the park.

World's Largest Tire

Bladenboro   34.55253° -78.78449°

Robert Hester started small. In 1963 he began his business with one truck that he drove and repaired himself. But he wanted to be big. So he grew his company into a truck shipping and repair business, hauling freight all around the east coast, and doing repairs on his trucks and any others that needed fixing. With the addition of his two sons, Hester Tire got big.

So it probably is fitting that they have the world's largest tire out in front of their building.

The 14 foot tall behemoth sits mounted on a base outside the tire and truck repair location on the outskirts of Bladenboro. The tire is meant for the Caterpillar built 797 dump truck, a giant hauler meant only for the biggest of mining and construction applications. The truck can carry up to 400 tons of material, along with supporting its own weight of 1,375,000 pounds. So the tires required for this beast must be hardy indeed. One tire is almost 12,000 pounds and 5 and a half feet wide, with a cost of around $42,500 each. Six tires are required for the big 797, so tire manufacturer Michelin makes a pretty penny every time one of those big trucks goes out.

Oddity ★

This is actually the world's largest real tire. The tires that are larger, including Uniroyal's giant radial in Michigan, are just stylized pieces of art. The Uniroyal tire used to be a Ferris Wheel.

Difficulty ★

It sits in front of Hester Tire, with the company's name on it, at an intersection outside of Bladenboro. Keep an eye on traffic while driving. Go in the daytime so you won't get tired.

The tires and axle assembly for the big 797 are both Carolina products. The axles are made in Winston-Salem, and the tires are made in South Carolina.

Bladenboro is also famous for a near mythical creature that once attacked a bunch of dogs. It was given the rather sanguine name of the Vampire Beast.

Gravity Hill

Laurinburg   34.70560° -79.42018°

Gravity Hills, while not common, are less rare than one might seem. There are a few in North Carolina alone. The Laurinburg Gravity Hill has its own special causes, reasons, and legends.

At the end of Stewartsville Cemetery Road, where it meets Old Maxton Road at an intersection, is the nexus of Gravity Hill. A car stopped at the intersection, if left in neutral, will slowly roll back up the hill, out of the intersection. No outside intervention moves the car. It merely rolls out of the way.

It is a simple act, but of course there is more to the story. Legend tells that years ago, at the same intersection, a car drifted into the road and was hit by a truck. A young girl was killed in the accident. The spirit lingers in the area, always ready to protect others from the same fate. If a car coasts into the intersection, she will come and push the car back away from the danger.

The reality is less exciting, but in this case, the reality is also a little less clear. Almost always, there is an optical illusion of sorts. Usually, a lack of a natural horizon fools the eye into thinking that a road that slopes one direction is flat, or actually slopes the opposite way. Sometimes there is also an artificial horizon, a hill nearby that creates a line that a viewer can imagine to be flat, but really is angled the opposite to the road. In the case of the Laurinburg gravity hill, it may be a mix of many things, including a tree line that may grow at a slight angle at the base of the road, near the intersection.

Whatever the cause, the effect is a little creepy. Visitors can try this out by stopping at the intersection of the roads, placing the car in neutral, and waiting for the car to back up. Fortunately, it only backs up a few feet, enough to get out of the intersection. However, be aware that other cars can be on the road; drivers don't want to be out of control of the car, or endanger anyone in testing this. Some people have even put the car in neutral and gotten out of the car to show that no one is interacting with it. This is highly discouraged. A car without someone to steer or stop can easily go off the road and be damaged or hit someone behind it.

Oddity ★★

The effect of Gravity Hill is always a little odd. Even your body feels like it is leaning forward when going back.

Difficulty ★★

Warnings about going there and doing this cannot be stressed enough. Other people could be there, out of their cars, no control on their vehicles, so don't expect someone to be able to get out of your way. Also, if you do try it, make sure you stay in the car, engine running, foot over the brake. Even turning the car off is dangerous, as the steering wheel can lock.

Boar's Nest Dukes of Hazzard Museum

Rougemont 36.27217° -78.88299°

In January of 1979, based on a successful B-movie of the mid 1970s, CBS launched, almost literally, a new show onto its viewers. *The Dukes of Hazzard* was a quick hit with fans. TV watchers were gifted with a down home southern charm from a mysterious balladeer, telling the tales of the Duke family, a Georgia clan with roots deep in the rolling hills, and deep into making moonshine. Elder brother Luke, a former marine and boxer, came up with the plans that he and younger girl crazy brother Bo implemented in order to confound and escape from the clutches of the corrupt and nefarious Boss Hogg, the controlling businessman and politician who owned much of Hazzard County, Georgia. Add to that a beautiful and kind sister Daisy, always sporting the shortest of denim shorts, and the wise Uncle Jesse Duke, patriarch of the Duke clan and homestead, and fans of the show would be treated to a weekly battle of home spun Robin Hoods fighting the inept corruption in their little town. The Dukes constantly battled Boss Hogg, along with his toady sheriff, the crooked Roscoe P. Coltraine, who would always be on the lookout for the Dukes, hoping to trap them in some way, always adding his trademark petulant laugh, "Kew kew kew!" at every turn. The show also included the stalwart and reluctant deputy Enos Strate, and the Dukes best friend and mechanic Cooter Davenport.

Of course, the reasons for watching the show were wide and varied. The handsome and rugged Duke boys were as popular with girls as Daisy was with boys at the time, and everyone loved to hear Uncle Jesse's homespun advice, as well as to see Boss Hogg and Roscoe get their comeuppance. But the biggest star of the show may not even have been a person. The Duke boys drove a suped up Dodge

Charger, set up as a stock car in bright orange with the numbers 01 on the welded shut doors, and a Confederate flag on the roof. Named the General Lee, the car, and its myriad copies over the years, performed some amazing stunts on the show, almost always culminating in a huge jump off a ramp, flying through the air, and landing hard, only to escape Roscoe in his own Mopar vehicles (though early on, Roscoe drove an AMC Matador).

The show remained popular throughout its run, the formula never getting tired over its seven seasons. Other actors came and went, but the story lasted because it spoke to the core audience. Bo and Luke, on continual probation from running moonshine, fought with Boss Hogg to stop Hogg's infernal corruption. The rugged good guys that the Dukes were was portrayed in a unique way. Part of their probation meant that the boys could never carry rifles, and, being the modern Robin Hoods that they were, the Dukes would fight a Southern Prince John and his crooked sheriff with only bows and arrows.

The show made a lasting impression. As the number of broken Chargers piled up, and prices rose, the scarcity of the cars increased. Now an actual screen used General Lee can fetch a pretty penny. Even the cars that ended up with broken backs from the big jumps are worth easy six figure prices. But the cars aren't the only thing that made the show last.

Fans have kept the show alive. Tracey Duke is definitely a fan. He even chose the name of a long lost cousin to the Duke family for his own. In quiet Rougemont Dukes of Hazzard fans can come by and see a very good and very seriously well made replica of the Boar's Nest, the local watering hole on the show. Daisy worked the original Boar's Nest in a deal with Boss Hogg, and in return Hogg and Roscoe provided entertainment by entrapping the occasional country star to sing there. The Dukes of Hazzard museum here in Rougemont is a tribute to the show's time to slow down and enjoy a cold one after a week of driving dusty backroads and outwitting the law.

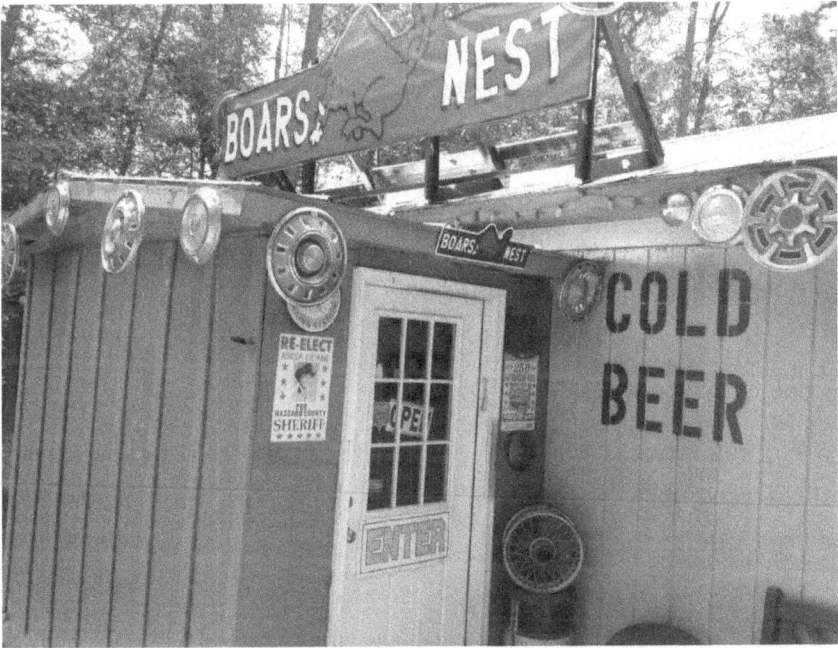

Tracey has the look down pat, with the hubcaps hanging outside, nearby a clothesline of Daisy's shorts hang out to dry. Inside the place has a seriously country feel, with Mason jars to prove it. Inside Waylon Jennings plays on the jukebox. Who else but the singer of the theme song and the balladeer himself would serenade fans? He has autographs from several of the show's stars, as well as memorabilia from the show, too. He's even got a Charger hidden around there somewhere.

Tracey is an interesting man to meet when you get there, too. He may be a good ol' boy, just like the Dukes, but he's also a bit of a geek, too. He works at the Museum of Life & Science in Durham for his regular job, and really loves what he does there, working with the displays that people see every day. And at the Boar's Nest, he has some things that the Dukes probably would never imagine (even though an alien did visit the Duke farm once.) Tracey may long to jump an orange Charger over a broken bridge, but he also likes to ride his homemade electric bicycles. And he is putting solar panels on the roof of the Boar's Nest. Boss Hogg would have hated that. He couldn't charge for electricity.

The Boar's nest museum is open Saturdays. It's easy to tell when you drive by. Just look for the big orange 01 flag hanging out front. There's no guarantee that Daisy will be working, though.

Oddity ★★

It's a great looking building, and pretty impressive how realistic it looks. Tracey really is a good ol' boy for doing this. And he's stayed on the right side of the law.

Difficulty ★★

You can drive up in your Charger, your old Ford 100, a Jeep with a golden eagle on it, but if you slide in there with blue lights flashing on your Plymouth Fury, the chase just might be on. Remember it is only open once a week, on Saturdays, usually.

Castle Mont Rouge

Rougemont 36.23957° -78.91301°

There is a strange and haunting magic hidden in old castles, with their tall turrets and parapets. Gargoyles guard and terrify, making the building upon which they perch even more foreboding. Even as the castles age, the ghosts still abide the rules. Who knows how long the magic of an old castle remains?

Maybe we can find out at Castle Mont Rouge.

A real castle was built in Rougemont by sculptor Richard Mihaly, a largely self-taught artist who once was the sculptor in residence at the Washington National Cathedral. Mihaly wanted a small and unique spot for his workshop, so he found a plot of land too steep to really build well up near Rougemont, where he began his castle. The building is not built in one specific style, with tall spires, onion domes of orthodox designs, and walls clad with marble. The cinder block construction was accented with wood floors.

Sadly, the sculptor halted construction. The castle wasn't abandoned, but just never completed on the inside. For a while Mihaly still used it as a workshop, but the castle fell into disrepair over time. Vandals came in and smashed out the windows, tagging the castle with graffiti. With the windows open to the elements, rain and cold came in, further damaging the building. Since no one was there to maintain the care of the place, the wood floors became rotten and falling in. Mihaly has tried to put the place up for sale, but with the unique care needed for the castle, and the difficulty of building on the land, no one has bought the place. Mihaly also tried to raise funds to repair the place, to no luck.

Now Castle Mont Rouge rises through the trees, worse for the wear, but still towering on the Red Mountain. Visiting the castle is not easy, and going inside is not a good idea. It sits at the top of the mountain, at the end of a steep, one mile long gravel one lane road, full of potholes and bumps. There are other homeowners up there, who will notice visitors (as well as anyone there for less altruistic purposes) and may call the sheriff on anyone who trespasses. Even if you go there, don't go inside. The interior is no longer safe. With the vandalism, the place is dangerous just to walk around, and who knows who could be lingering around the place. This property is well known, but still someone's private property. A visit from the road is okay, but don't go close looking for dragons.

Oddity ★★★★★

The castle rises through the trees, incongruous and sad, but still amazing. Most of the houses in and around Rougemont are common, regular. This one reaches up to the sky with tiny spires, a lost promise, a goal never met.

Difficulty ★★★★★

It's far off any paved road, and even having arrived, it sits in the trees and is difficult to see from the narrow gravel road. With all the negatives on this, the questionable safety, the privacy issues, the danger of running into a stranger, it would be best not to even go. If you do, just remember not to get too close and really keep an eye on your surroundings. Legally, you probably can drive up to the end of the road, but no farther. But even then, really, that road is scary. Don't go at night, don't go in the rain, don't go if you see some sketchy people, wizards, dragons, ogres...

Endor Furnace

Cumnock   35.55325° -79.21855°

North Carolina has been known for a lot of famous things. Many remember the phrase "Variety Vacationland," meant to show off the myriad choices visitors and natives alike had in recreation across the state. And residents always saw the plowed fields blooming with the floral children of the North Carolina farms, cotton and tobacco. Even before that, some may know that the Tar Heel State was the first place in the U.S. to find gold. But most may not know that North Carolina was also part of the growing coal and iron ore mining industry that kicked in the mid 1800s.

That is why in 1862 brothers John and Donald McRae, along with John Dix, moved from Wilmington into the middle of the state to begin mining. The start of the Civil War played no small part in their business as well. The Confederacy would need to begin industrialization from a largely agrarian economy, and would need iron and coal to feed the war. So the three men came to a spot in the wilderness that would become Lee County and built the Endor Iron Furnace, a giant iron kiln meant to melt down the ore mined some 10 miles away and turn it into pig iron.

The Endor furnace was built into the hill of the Deep River. The location was picked probably because it was close to the raw materials needed, the brownstone that was carved up and set into the chimney. The furnace is unique in that respect in that it has no mortar, as it would have leached into the molten iron. The stones were carved, but not just simply carved. They were shaped and beveled to give the furnace a special appearance. The furnace stands about 35 feet tall, with four sides, the bottom open with arches to allow the air to flow through the furnace. The raw ore and fuel would be dumped into the top from the bank of the river to allow it to heat and melt, with the resultant iron and slag poured off at the bottom.

The furnace was probably located in this spot because it was easier to build it near the source of the brownstone, though it was far away from the iron ore. The ore was brought to the furnace and refined, then shipped off from a train spur that would run to Fayetteville, taking the pig iron to places farther afield to be used for the war effort. Endor operated for the duration of the war, until 1865. It went dormant until 1870, when it was used again for a brief period of time. Afterwards, it was abandoned to nature.

And nature took its course. For about 130 years the furnace sat uncared for, but known. Only recently did the residents of Lee and Chatham counties, and the citizens of nearby Sanford, take a more direct hand in a location they had mostly just heard about, or maybe had hiked to on occasion. The locals have raised money to begin the attempt to preserve and repair the furnace, as well as to create a state park.

Right now, the Endor Furnace still sits as it was, slowly succumbing to the kiss of nature. But it has been cared for to an extent. The place is historically important. Very few places from the 1860s still exist in their original form, or at least original pieces. It is a marker to our past, majestic in its bulk and its silent power. It may no longer burn, but visitors can imagine the heat it made when functioning.

Oddity ★★

The Endor Furnace is a towering piece of masonry, and it's a nice hike, too. No campfires in the furnace.

Difficulty ★★★★

You gotta park the car and hike. You like to hike, don't you? (You also have to hike back.) Take some water. There are a few spots at the end of the road to leave a vehicle, and the gate is closed to traffic, but walking up to the furnace from the gated end of the road is allowed. There are some warning signs, but they only remind people not to take things from the area. Also, it's a lonely spot. Some visitors may want to travel in groups.

HartleyHenge

Chapel Hill 35.94064° -79.10943°

Druids.

Okay, no, it's not Druids. It probably is an even more interesting story. Certainly it is a story about a very interesting man. The Stonehenge type spiral built into Stone Knoll, a newer housing development near Chapel Hill, is only a small part of a tale of a well known man who lived in Carrboro, and built homes for the people that lived there.

John Hartley was an architect and developer in Carrboro, who was responsible for several subdivisions in the area. He left his mark, both physically in the case of HartleyHenge, as well as socially. While most developments attack the land, clearing and flattening it so that as many houses can be built in the space as possible, Hartley would do the opposite. He would examine the land, letting it determine how the house would be built. His homes would have a south facing front, in order to let in the sun and moon throughout the day and night. He would go on medicine walks, linking himself with the land, and build from the ground up. His home design followed the philosophy of Frank Lloyd Wright, believing that the home and land should be in agreement, that they should grow together.

Many of his homes are impressive in that they have a large amount of trees on them, rather than being cleared of any vertical life. The homes are almost hidden by nature, they are so nestled into the native land. He even took that belief into developing entire neighborhoods. All the subdivisions he built have a communal space within them. Among the things he has placed in his developments are a labyrinth and an amphitheater. It is his way to get the residents out of their houses and into the land where they live. He creates a sense of community and awareness in his designs.

For Stone Knoll, he built a spiral henge monument. Rocks create a spiral path, with four large obelisks on the cardinal directions of the compass. Each tall obelisk is a totem for Hartley. He described them thusly. The eastern obelisk is the eagle, a symbol of the rising sun. The south has the coyote and represents noon. The west is the bear and the setting of the sun. The northern obelisk is the white buffalo and old age.

HartleyHenge is open to the public, as it is a public area for the residents. Visitors are welcome to come see the henge, as long as they are respectful, realizing that this is really the community's property.

Oddity ★★

Even the spiral blends into the land. It is noticeable from the road, but also easily missed. It is a good tribute to the idea that Hartley had of bringing the homeowners together with the land they occupied.

Difficulty ★★

A small spot for off the street parking is available right off the road in the subdivision. Park and walk the short path to the henge. The area has some simple rules for visiting, so be respectful of the regulations.

The obelisks were not mined nearby. They were actually castoff from a quarry in Tennessee. The stones were all trucked in for the henge.

Center Of The State

Star   35.39975° -79.75666°

Star was the center of North Carolina before it became the center of North Carolina.

Huh?

Okay, it may not make much sense at first, but it will. Star was founded in 1897, after several decades of growth when gold was discovered in the area. Star was a center for mining, lumber and bricks, so it didn't take long for the railroad lines to build into the town. The Aberdeen and Asheboro Railroad was later met with the Durham and Charlotte Railroad, creating a junction in Star. The Leach family built a hotel in the town to serve the workers on the railroad as well as travelers passing through. Often, people riding the trains would have to get off one line, then spend the night, wake up to have breakfast, and get on a train going on a different railroad. The hotel became essentially a bed and breakfast, offering a place to sleep and a quick bite for travelers before sending them on their way. The hotel still is open as the Star Hotel Bed and Breakfast, and still serves people using Star as a central point to visit places nearby.

Thanks to the rail lines, more industry moved into Star. In addition to lumber, Star produced turpentine, furniture, and other products. A bottling plant came to the town, and hosiery mills opened in Star. The town grew through the first half of the twentieth century with all the new jobs. With all those trains coming in, Star became a hub for transportation throughout North Carolina. It was place not only for trains and freight to move and sort themselves, but also a place for people to get from one place to another. It truly became the center of the state. More recently, the mills have closed down and the town looks for new industry to come in and bring more employment to the area.

Star was named a U.S. Postal Service Christmas Town, and now postmarks thousands of Christmas cards and letters every December. Each year a stamp is designed from a contest held with the citizens of Star. Letters come in, get stamped by the postmaster, and go out all over the country.

But Star became most famous for being the geographic center of the state. When looking at Star's location on a map, it doesn't look quite dead center in the middle of North Carolina. Raleigh looks more like it is in the middle of the state. That is due to how deceptively long North Carolina is, as well as the varying degrees of thickness from north to south. Star sits where a line halfway across the state would meet a line halfway down the state. The actual location is just east of town, in a field near a lake on private property. There is a simple plaque that marks the location. Going to the plaque requires permission.

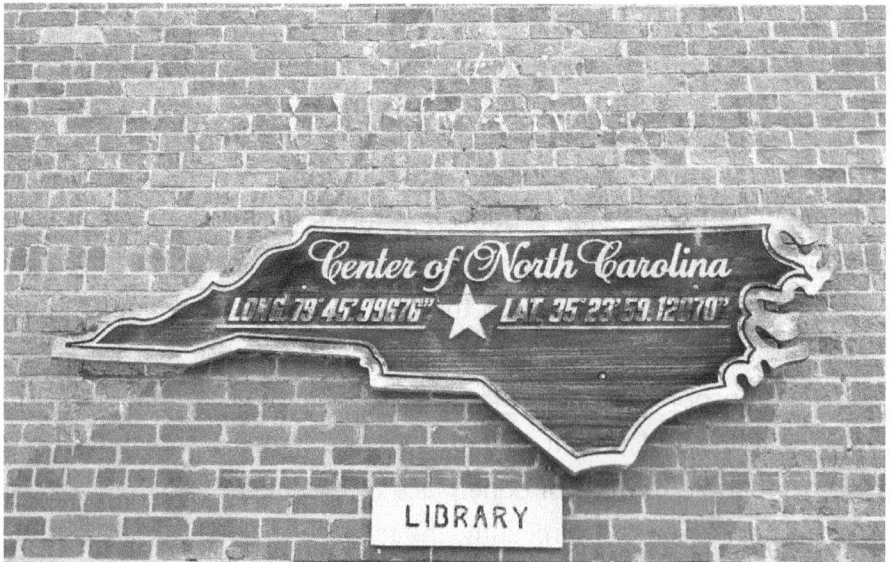

Oddity ★

The oddest thing is that Star wasn't named for being a star on the map as the center of the state.

Difficulty ★★★★

Going to see the plaque is difficult, as it is on private land. Visiting Star is easy, though. It's a nice little town, another Mayberry in the state to visit for a while.

Due to all the growth in the town, in the 1960s Star was one of the first towns in the state to build public housing.

Arnold Freeman Art Field

Eagle Springs 35.35698° -79.65199°

This place is pretty good work for a self taught welder. Arnold Freeman started piecing together bits of metal when he needed a mailbox. He put it up in the front of a field at his home in the little township of Eagle Springs, near Zion Grove and Biscoe. That was the start of his art field. He continued with the idea of filling it up with 100 art pieces.

He's got about 400 or 500 now. So much for restraint.

Arnold saw welders working and decided he liked it, so at 24 he taught himself how to weld, and turned his desire into a job. So in between his repair work, working on the lawnmowers that cut the fine grass at Pinehurst's greens, he found bits and pieces to put together to make some seriously heavy metal art.

Every piece has a name to it. Every piece is something he saw in a piece of metal that he could make in to something more. He has animals and people, from the generic to the specific. A golfer has graced his yard for a while now, made of the old reels and blades of a mower fittingly used at Pinehurst. It is something that is deceptively simple, to personify an inanimate object.

Freeman's objects are sometimes smaller than other big metal sculptures, but that just means he has time to make more of them. When the grass grows, the tall plants sometimes hide a few of the smaller pieces, and that just makes it more fun to find what is hidden.

Visiting the field is not difficult, but it is rather out of the way. Going there just to see the field may be a bit of a disappointment, but passing by during a road trip may bring a reward. The property has some Do Not Enter signs up, which are meant to keep people from driving into the homes behind the field, but pulling over right in front is okay.

Oddity ★★

Art fields are nice things to run into on a drive, and a stop is always recommended. A lot of these pieces are based off of found art ideas, the vision of someone to see more in a simple item than what others see. A bit of scrap to most of us becomes a head, eye, hair, nose, or arm to Freeman.

Difficulty ★

It is right by the road, though it is a little in the middle of nowhere. That just makes a stop for visitors more likely. Why else would anyone be out there? Go ahead, take a look. A few of the pieces might even be for sale. Pick one up, as the outsider art movement doesn't part with many works very often.

Giant Mosquito

Asheboro 35.70555° -79.81553°

AAAAAAAAAAAAAAAAAAAAAAAAAAAAAAAAAAAAAAAAAAAAAHH!!!!

Oddity ★★★★

Okay, we don't grow'em quite that big here in NC.

Difficulty ★

It's a good place to park and walk through the town. Don't forget your insect repellant.

Giant Shuttle

Glencoe   36.13842° -79.42760°

North Carolina turned quickly to textiles and millwork after the Civil War and Reconstruction in order to find new industry and jobs. The Haw River around Burlington was especially well suited for water power. In 1880, William and James Holt built Glencoe Village and Cotton Mill. The Holt brothers were the sons of E.M. Holt, founder of the Alamance Factory, which was the first mill in the South to dye yarn and make plaid. The mill was a family tradition.

Mills needed lots of workers, a steady stream of human power to match the steady stream of the Haw running next to the mill. Glencoe Village was built along the ridge near the bank of the river. About half of the 500 mill workers lived within the company village, in nearly identical houses, where they paid 50 cents a week rent for the house and a plot of land for farming. In addition, a company store and a school were part of the community. The school was important to James Holt. He insisted that the children in the village attend school for a certain amount of time before working at the mill. Yes, children worked at the mill, making 40 cents a day. Men earned one to two dollars a day, working 66 hours a week. Women earned about half that. Day wages would go up by the turn of the century, and hours would be cut back to only 63 hours a week, working 6 days a week.

This may seem harsh, with long hours, relatively low pay, children working, and the company shop taking the same money they just paid out, but at the time, the people that worked there enjoyed the community and the steady work. A job meant a roof over their family's head, and food in the oven, and food in the belly. For most of the mill workers, the job was much better than the unsure farm life they left behind.

The mill provided steady work for decades. While working for something akin to sharecropping, with token pay, and controlled rentals, with questionable oversight, there still was enough of a benefit to working at the water powered looms day in and day out. In the summer, the water on the Haw would run low, and work would shutter for an hour or two. The down time meant no pay, but to the workers, a few hours off in the summer was like a vacation. They would spend time catching up on chores, fishing or swimming in the river, and socializing with their coworkers. When the water began to run again, so did the looms, and the people went back to work.

The mill and the people would work until 1954. By that time there was too much competition from other mills, and many were being consolidated into larger factories. Almost all the workers left immediately to find new jobs. Only a few stayed.

The few that did stay led to a rather undeserving and insulting legend in the area. The Massey family remained in the village for years afterward. The parents had five children while working at the mill. While the two oldest were born and grew up healthy, three younger siblings were born with what probably was brittle bone disease. Pete Massey was healthy enough to go to school, but his siblings Thelma and Donnie were confined to wheelchairs, their bones too weak to support them. They were resigned to sit on the front porch, day after day, while they waited for their brother to come home. Due to their disease, they never grew tall. In the 1950s, there was little in the world that was more teased than someone different. The Massey children, stuck on a porch, became the target of torment. Teenagers would drive out to see the kids, trapped at home, making fun of them. Soon, older brother Pete made sure they were prepared to fight back. He would pile up rocks for Thelma and Donnie to throw at anyone who came by to gawk at them. Unfortunately, the legend got written by the people that went back to town, telling of how the little people of Glencoe would assault them, just for driving through. The legend of "Munchkinland" was born.

It didn't matter that the Massey family was actually very nice churchgoing people, or that they were the victims of bullies. The legend told the tale. Now people feared going into Glencoe, that the people there would shoot at them, chase the cars down, pull them out and beat them. Even though the Masseys moved away in 1960, the legend lived on. Once the village was abandoned, it became inhabited by a different set of residents. The area was home to vagrants, drugs, and even became a popular Lover's Lane due to the isolation and lack of desire for anyone to go there to look out for the place.

Glencoe Village had to wait until 1997 for something positive to come along. Preservation North Carolina purchased the land and began the preservation of the homes and mill, and later the area was turned into a local historical district. The houses were sold to people who wanted to restore them to a period look, while at the same time adding to them and upgrading the homes for today's family needs. Now the village looks restored and preserved. It is a very complete mill town, one of the most well preserved in the state. The houses are homes to families and retired couples, all content to live in a peaceful little community. And the quaintness has paid off, literally. The homes are now highly valued as pieces of history, and command high prices, if they go up for sale at all.

The mill was purchased by Hedgehog Holdings, a North Carolina property development company. The mill buildings are being converted over to private use for apartments and businesses. The main mill floor is still closed for renovation. It sits empty of looms, but full of stories. A giant central wooden beam runs the ceiling. A large hardwood beam wouldn't burn in case of a fire; it would char and still hold the roof up, an early safety feature that would help preserve the mill.

A visit to Glencoe now is a much more leisurely journey. It is not only home to the many quaint houses, but several other interesting places to visit. The Textile Heritage Museum is adjacent to the mill, and across the street is the superintendant's house. The Superintendant had a few benefits in living there. The house, though similar to the others, was a little bigger, with a large wraparound porch, and it was the closest to the mill. It also allowed a clear view of the village, so the superintendant could keep an eye on the workers in their off time. Preservation NC also has a small satellite office in the village. The village is a group of private homes, so visiting in one is not possible, but visiting the museum is. It is open on the weekends from 1-4.

There are also some private businesses to see there, an antique store, some artist collectives, and offices. Parking is easy. Just park by the giant shuttle.

In tribute to the workers of the mill, Steve Cote created a gigantic metal shuttle and bobbins to be displayed in front of the mill. A shuttle normally is fairly small, meant to be held in one hand and flicked between the strands of yarn on a loom to carry the thread back and forth, creating the cloth. The shuttle was ubiquitous in a mill, as common as a hammer in a tool chest. This shuttle is much bigger, and won't even fit in a house. Propped up on two bobbins to help it stand up, the shuttle is a much larger version of the boat shuttles used long ago. With the village's water tower as a backdrop, it makes a nice photo opportunity. No thread, so no one is going to be making any giant plaid blankets with it, but it sure looks cool.

Oddity ★★★

The shuttle is both a well fitting tribute to the mill and the workers that lived there, as well as a strange modern, clean piece of art in a town that is so well preserved for being so old. It fits in, and stands out.

Difficulty ★

Next to the gravel parking lot at the mill, it is hard to miss. But the town is small, quiet, and quaint. Drive slowly when going. And the mill itself is being renovated, with some areas closed, out of reach or unsafe. Don't to exploring near the river. The old mill power plant is now used to generate electric power, which makes another place off limits. But don't worry, all the cool stuff can be seen in the town. The museum is only open the afternoon on weekends, but go in the morning if you can; the early light looks nice on the houses.

North Carolina is rightly famous for its mills and fabrics. The Tar Heel state has its own plaid, or tartan, designed in 1981, and based on a pattern worn by King Charles II when he was crowned king of Scotland. The Carolinas were chartered by him, and named after his father, Charles I.

Erwin, NC hosts Denim Days to honor their mill heritage. They used to have the world's largest pair of blue jeans on display, but they went missing when the mill closed and the company, Swift Denim, moved out of state.

Alamance County was where the first pair of stretchable nylon stockings for women was invented. Before, stores had to carry specific sizes of nylons, with the seams up the back.

Chris-Chris

Burlington   36.10961° -79.39216°

Hidden along the rolling water of the Haw River in Burlington is a creature so vicious, so hideous, that for decades no person would set foot upon the island where he lives. On the now abandoned Goat Island, the largest island in the Haw, resides Chris-Chris, a bigfoot like creature with a taste for goats and children.

The legend began with a tale of a mean old man who lived on Goat Island. He raised his goats alone. He liked being alone. Besides being alone and raising goats, he seems to have hated everything else. Especially children. Legend tells that kids visiting the island would not return. On the island there was a bottomless pool or well, and that was not only where this evil goat man hid his victims, but also where he was thrown when the townsfolk found out what he was doing. The locals came over, got the guy, and did something unspeakable to him. Or, at least, half of him.

Soon, a half human, half monster creature was spotted coming from Goat Island. This Bigfoot monster had the taste for deer, and a pretty sour attitude. People exploring along the Haw would occasionally find a deer, killed and partially eaten, a victim of Chris-Chris, along the trails near Goat Island.

The legend became a little more mellow, with just a large Bigfoot who liked to eat deer wandering the woods, and living on the island, while the gory and murderous human tale drifted away on the waters of the Haw River. Thank goodness. Chris-Chris appeared rarely, often just seen from his footprint or the occasional dead animal that must have been victim of Chris-Chris' diet, for no other excuse could explain a dead animal by the river, of course.

Now, happily, Chris-Chris has even removed venison from his diet. It seems the "monster" has found a more preferred meal, and a nicer place to eat than the side of a river. Chris-Chris had his first taste of Zack's Hot Dogs, and he won't go back to hunting deer. Now he heads to downtown Burlington when he's hungry, and gets a couple.

Now, everything in this story is absolutely true. Well, the legend is, but all that stuff is actually made up. Want to know the real story? Read on. Just want to scare the kids at the campfire? Skip to the next part. So, yes, the legend is real. There really was a tale of a Bigfoot-like, half human, half beast creature that lived on Goat Island.

But that's all, just a tale. The reality is that Chris-Chris was created, allegedly by some moonshiners who had set up a still on the island. Goat Island is a large island in the middle of the Haw, about a mile long. It was good for being out of the way, being hidden, and most people would have a hard time getting there. Which made it perfect for cooking whiskey. So a dead deer was placed near the island, and Chris-Chris the legend was born. It was great for scaring away anyone who might want to come snooping.

Goat Island did have a house on it at some time, but the home burned down to the foundation long ago. There is a bridge that leads over to the island, but it is not safe to cross. There are the remains of the house somewhere on the island, but it may be best not to go searching. That bottomless pit may be there, too.

Oddity ★★

It's a kind of strange, creepy, scary looking place. The house burned down, and the fire department wouldn't even go over to put the fire out. Either it was too scary, or the bridge wouldn't hold.

Difficulty ★★★★★

While the island is the largest in the river, it can only be seen up close by paddling out to the location. Unsafe for a lot of reasons, private property, rickety bridge, who knows who is wandering around, scary monsters... goats... Only visit if you have the skills to handle a kayak, and can be sure of your safety. Maybe take a couple of hot dogs, just in case.

Muffler Man

Burlington   36.09824° -79.43447°

Now, there are muffler men, and then there's this muffler man.

Muffler men were fiberglass statues, large cast figures of a man perfect to hold giant mufflers, made by International Fiberglass of Venice, CA. The men were about 25 feet tall, with separate parts for heads and arms, so that they could be personalized. But all were about the same type, a big guy with a beard, looming over a car repair place, one hand upturned, the other hand over, in a strange frozen pose that only looked right if they were holding a big muffler, exhaust pipes in each hand.

This one is really a muffler man. He's a man made out of mufflers. At least 21 of them. AIM Mufflers and Exhaust Systems built this guy out of mufflers as a bit of roadside art to help promote their services. They also have a car built like a giant muffler.

Oddity ★★★★

It's a pretty creative way to advertise your services. He's got a smiling face, with a long nose, but you still can't tell how it smells. He's pretty quiet, too.

Difficulty ★

Even though their parking lot may get filled up with cars they are working on, there is a lot across the street from the sculpture. Church Street, where it is located, is a busy road. Be careful driving and parking. You are welcomed to come take a look. AIM Mufflers even say, "No Appointment Necessary – We'll Hear You Coming."

Garden Railroad

Gibsonville   36.10509° -79.54068°

Every traveler knows that the road plays a song for them. There is a regular beat that calls out a time to whoever journeys across the land. In North Carolina, we say the road and we know what that means. It's the miles and miles of blacktop from the mountains to the sea, from north to south, and every little Mayberry town in between.

But that wasn't always the case. For a long time, North Carolina had terrible streets, so bad that they could stop even the Civil war from encroaching farther inland than the reach of the rivers. And the first roads were quite literally tobacco roads, where barrels of tobacco leaf would be rolled to market, beating down the best path to town.

So when some people said "The Road," they didn't mean a paved road, or a dirt road. They meant the railroad.

Bobby Summers says "The Road."

Summers was a train guy, a real train guy, from way back when. He joined Norfolk Southern, working the rail yards, or as he says, "the Yard," in 1959. He soon moved into the Road, and worked as a conductor until July 4, 1992. Over the years, he gathered his share of stories. And so did his wife, Peggy.

One time Bobby got called to do a job on a train, and he had the keys. Peggy, then a young mom with three kids, contacted him to get the keys. So she waited by the depot for him to come by on his train. At 3 a.m. As she's waiting in the dark, a police officer pulls up and asks what she's doing. She responds simply, "Waiting for a train." The police officer, probably unsure of what to do, said, "Well, I'll wait with you." So at 3:30 in the morning, a train pulls up, the caboose gets to the depot and stops, and Bobby comes out and tosses her the keys.

Another time she had to deliver Bobby a change of clothes, so again, they ran the train through the town to stop in Gibsonville. At least the caboose stopped there. The engine stopped in neighboring Elon.

So Bobby worked the Road until he was ready to retire. But it was obviously hard to get him out of trains. Summers retired into a couple of hobby stores, selling model kits and scale trains. He now owns Bobby's Hobbies and Bobby's World of Trains. Running the smaller scales is probably easier for Bobby than the full size ones he used to ride as a conductor. Soon, however, he became interested in the larger scale models. The big G scale trains are fun and detailed, due to their large size, but also can take up a lot of room. The little HO trains of kids' rooms are tiny in comparison. These large scale trains can be set up out in a garden area where they really can spread out. Which is exactly what Bobby did.

He went to the town and asked if he could build a large train set in the community greens where the old depot used to be. Gibsonville thought it would be a great idea, so Bobby set about building it. People would come by and see him, laying track, or putting up bricks for something. Sometimes they would ask him,

"What are you building?" His answer? "Wall." And if he left a space for a tunnel, well that was just where he ran out of bricks. He ended up with over 1500 feet of track out in the courtyard, room for several trains to run. He even built a version of the Golden Gate Bridge as part of his display. The local newspaper was happy to run an article on how the Golden Gate Bridge was now in Gibsonville.

So Bobby Summers got his trains installed in 1997, and they have been running ever since. It usually runs during special events and on weekends in the summer, depending on the weather. Just seeing the track is pretty impressive, too. It's a nice little, well, not so little village with a lot of detail. Bobby recently sold the track to a new operator, as it was getting more difficult for him to get out there and keep it cleaned up and running, but visitors can still see the trains going on occasion. And if not, well, the town also has a caboose as its railroad museum, open every day to tour for free. And Bobby got them that caboose, too. He simply went to his old boss and asked for one. And they ended up with a caboose Bobby actually used when he was working on The Road.

Oddity ★★

It really is a fancy and well made model town, with 1500 feet of track to see. Of course, it looks even better when the different trains are running. Three or four engines pulling loads can easily fit onto the tracks.

Difficulty ★★

The track is easily seen by parking downtown and going up to the fence, but the trains only run occasionally. Since the town owns the land, they may be able to tell visitors when the trains will be running. Weekends or special events are better times.

Tiny Lutheran Church

Gibsonville   36.12931° -79.56626°

Tiny churches are a staple of the backroads of America. It seems that no matter where the road takes you, there will be some place, big or small, to give your soul a little rest. Small churches are built for many reasons. Some are built just to define a spot, to be a building on a piece of land used for services. Some are labors of love by a single person, while others are bigger tributes from an entire community.

In this case, the Friedens tiny church was built in remembrance of the original log church built on the same property long ago. The first Lutheran church was built in 1745 as a log church. It was built by German settlers to the area, who had been moving into North Carolina for over 70 years. The original church was known as "Sshaaker's Church," which later changed to the more Anglicized Shoemaker's Church. By 1868, the parishioners decided to start making bricks for a more sturdy structure, and then built a new church on the site, the third structure that served the congregation. The hand made nature of the bricks was discovered later in 1939 when the church almost burned down in a fire. The brick columns, the frame of the church, were all that survived. In the rubble was found one of the original bricks, complete with a dog's paw print where the animal ran across the soft clay before it hardened.

With all the building, rebuilding, and additions the Friedens did, it's no wonder they built a little church on the side of the property. It's just a little building, but it serves its purpose. It is made of the logs hewn for the original log church, with the chinking sealing the walls from the outside. Open the door and find two rows of pews, room for about eight people to sit, as well as a simple light and altar. Even though it is old and grey, it still holds a simple majesty, like the original church probably had, too. The new church of brick may be a little sturdier, more sound, but the tiny church sure has charm.

Oddity ★★★

It may seem normal to have a church on church property, but this certainly has a unique look. It is a very photogenic little building. Maybe not the place to do a baptism, but...

Difficulty ★

Park across the street at the church. Even though the road is not busy, look both ways and use the crosswalk! Also, there is a somewhat abandoned decorative well nearby. Watch your step, hold on to your children. Make sure Lassie is with you, "What is it, girl? Dad's trapped? Down a well?"

Elvis Ate Here

Whitsett   36.06900° -79.58748°

Elvis probably ate just about everywhere. Anywhere that would deep fry a peanut butter and banana sandwich. Elvis became famous for his high food intake, and his passion for rich foods. As a young man, touring meant doing a lot of his own road work. Days were long, and the concerts were grinding. Most rockers probably burned more than they ate, and Elvis knew how to shake those calories off better than anybody.

In 1956, Elvis was a big regional star, already famous, and rich, with a $40,000 contract from RCA and several new future hits that he had just recorded. He would soon be a national star, but right now he had to tour to promote his songs, to get them on the radio and get kids buying them. He began a tour of the east coast in Virginia, with two dates in the Tidewater region, before heading to Wilson for a show. He toured with his band, The Blue Moon Boys, but also with a host of other musicians, including Mother Maybelle and the Carter Sisters, among other bluegrass and country performers. After performing in Wilson, Elvis drove his 1955 Cadillac, the car later to go down in history, to Burlington, where he checked in after midnight. Having nothing much to do until his show that night, Elvis puttered around town, trying to get his new song, That's Alright Mama, played on local radio. The song didn't fit in with the local radio station's sound. Elvis then went to a local record store and tried to give out free tickets, discounts, and sell some of his records. He had little luck there as well.

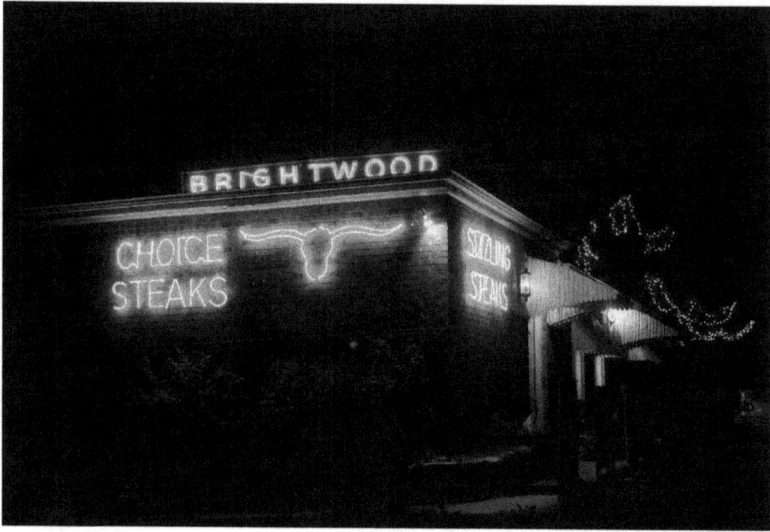

Elvis performed at Williams High School to a large crowd. However, many people in Burlington were there to see the other performers, and left when Elvis came on. The locals were not used to or ready for Elvis' gyrations and rocking sound. Some girls hung around after the show to see if they could get his autograph. They found him flirting with a young blonde at the upstairs women's restroom. After chatting with him and getting his signature, they departed. Elvis, too, had to move on. At some time, Elvis had left the building.

The next show was in Winston-Salem, which meant another late drive in the Cadillac. And a late dinner. Elvis and several others in the tour pulled into the Brightwood Inn for something to eat. There waitress Louise Little remembers him getting a hamburger with lettuce and tomato, with a glass of milk. She also remembered there being a woman with him, a young blonde.

Today the table sits as a shrine of sorts. Elvis ate here. The old Brightwood hasn't changed too much. It still is a long brick building with old booths and a bar with swivel chairs so that patrons can belly up to the old Formica countertop. It originally opened as a drive in back in 1936, a place with car hops to come out and meet patrons behind the wheel. The novelty of the place is in more than the Elvis table. Behind the counter there is an enormous amount of bric-a-brac, strange collectibles and items brought in by the owner and his guests. Paul Treadway has owned the place since before Elvis came in. It still is a local watering hole, and offers up steaks from cows raised on a nearby ranch.

So, if you are a fan of the King, stop by for lunch or dinner, take some change for the jukebox, and have a cold one in the Elvis booth.

Oddity ★

The booth is still set up as a tribute, and the whole place is a bit of a throwback to simpler times, where a stop on the road really meant a stop.

Difficulty ★

The Brightwood is open for lunch and dinner. Bright neon welcomes drivers as they crest a small ridge on highway 70, a welcome sight for many a hungry traveler in years past.

Note: I can neither recommend nor dissuade people from where they eat. This is for entertainment purposes only. Just like going into a spooky old place, I don't know what you will be getting into wherever you go get a bite. –J.S.

Solar System Walk

Jamestown   35.99927° -79.91573°

Everyone has seen those little Styrofoam models of the solar system. A collection of scratchy white balls, some colorful paint, and a few wires is all the budding astronomer needs to create an exact replica of the planets that orbit our sun. Each planet is the same distance away from the next, just a few inches, and they all orbit the sun in a perfect line. They are even easier to make now that Pluto has been put out to pasture as a planet (poor Pluto.)

The only problem with those things is that they get everything wrong. That was probably one of the things that set Aaron Martin, an instructor at Guilford Technical Community College, on the path to creating a Solar System Walk on his campus. He and Dr. Donald Cameron, president of the college, had seen other solar walks at different campuses, and thought it would be a good addition to GTCC. Not only would it be an attractive addition to the walking paths, it also serves as a more accurate map of the solar system, especially for kids who come to visit the campus to see the planets and other celestial bodies, and their relation to the sun.

Based on the scale that the Earth is 15 meters from the Sun, with the Sun being represented at the Cline Observatory dome, home of the campus' 24-inch telescope, the planets and other important celestial bodies in the solar system stretch out 1,800 meters across the campus. Each planet is represented by a plaque, with images and information about the planets on them. Visitors are welcome to tour the walk when campus is open. It is a short stroll, with one road to cross. The campus is beautiful in spring with the trees blooming.

Oddity ★

It's not strange in any way, just unique. Each planet and some other bits in the solar system are represented. If the college offers any open house programs to look through the telescope, that would be a great time to go. If the skies are clear and dark enough.

Difficulty ★★

Parking during the week may be an issue if the students are there. Weekends and evenings find the lots pretty empty. There is a walking path that leads to the observatory.

Giant Coffee Pot

Stokesdale   36.23560° -79.95879°

First of all, it is a giant coffee pot. It has been referred to as a tea pot, but no mistake, it's a coffee pot. Why? Well, because that's what everyone in Stokesdale know it as. Perhaps it has been named a tea pot to distinguish it from the big coffee pot in Old Salem, made by the Mickey brothers. Considering that this one is probably bigger than the Winston-Salem pot, they can call it whatever they want.

Sitting in front of Countryside Retirement Village, it is a nice decorative addition to their sign. It has no particular significance to the business, but it does have some personal attachment. And some mystery. To keep the mystery, at least for a little while, let's work backwards on how the coffee pot got there.

Sometime in the late 1980s or early 1990s, Dr. Mervyn King of Countryside Retirement saw that the restaurant across the street was going to be torn down. Cook's Restaurant had been closed for years, and had been leasing their space to other tenants. When the building needed to be torn down, he acquired the coffee pot, and he and his son-in-law, Steve Edgerton took the thing and refurbished it. The pot is made of zinc, and will not rust, but the parts that hold it together would. So they fixed it up, painted it, and placed it across the street from the restaurant at the retirement community. It was a little more roundabout than that; they

had to take it home to Virginia to work on it, then bring it back to Stokesdale. Now it sits as a cool roadside attraction, a preserved landmark, and a pretty nice sign.

But how did it get on the restaurant?

In the late 1950s, after William and Evelyn Cook had opened a restaurant called Cook's Restaurant, they wanted to purchase the coffee pot to put on their building. Evelyn had been seeing the coffee pot in a field in the Sedgefield area of Greensboro, far to the south. It just sat there, in a state of disrepair, so she bought it. She said they didn't pay much for it. After moving it, repairing the pot, and hiring a crane to install it on their restaurant, it became a landmark for their place. It was a promise to drivers on Highway 158 that they could get a cuppa Joe, a bite to eat, and probably a bit of conversation about the big coffee pot on the roof.

One particularly interesting conversation was remarkably short. A man came in to the restaurant and asked about the coffee pot. He told Evelyn he was from Burlington, and had known the person who made it. He said it was much older than they thought, and was actually made sometime in the late 1800s.

And this is where the mystery begins. A long way away from an answer of where the coffee pot came from and how it ended up in a field in Sedgefield, then on top of a restaurant, and finally in front of a retirement community. Was the pot made for an advertisement for a place somewhere south of Greensboro? Why was it abandoned? Who made it? Where was it made? Those answers will have to be discovered sometime in the future.

The coffee pot happily has found a loving home, at least. It could have been sold several times when it was on Cook's, but it took the dismantling of the building under it to get the coffee pot moved. It's about ten feet tall, making it bigger than the Mickey pot in Winston-Salem by about three feet. So if you really need a morning wake up, go by Stokesdale first.

Oddity ★★

Sometimes companies used larger than life signs and objects to advertise what they made, often for customers who would recognize a shape, but not read a sign. This coffee pot is a survivor of a time long gone by, and a mystery to boot.

Difficulty ★

Keep your job, you don't need to retire to see it. The coffee pot is next to the retirement community sign. Pull into the road to take a picture. You may need to bring your own mug.

Ghost Lights

A Did You See That? Detour

North Carolina may not have a monopoly on ghost lights, but it very well may have the majority of them. Ghost lights, especially lights that appear around train tracks, are a virtual staple of the state. There could be numerous reasons for the lights appearing along the old rail lines. Some lights may be caused by a strange and unique attraction between the metal rails and a change in electrical current in the air, especially during or after a storm. Other causes may be from ball lightning or will-o'-the-wisp, a strange gaseous ignition that happens around marshes and heavy organic matter. Still, it could simply be that there are just so many train conductors losing their heads all the time.

The most famous of the North Carolina ghost lights is the Maco Light, inland from Wilmington, near the small town of Maco. Vacationers used to make a regular stop of the old train tracks to see the light, and they saw it regularly. There was less a question of whether or not one would see the Maco Light, and more just how close they could get. The Maco Light was attributed to Joe Baldwin, a train conductor who lost his head in an accident. His headless spirit still walked the rails looking for his head, or perhaps just still trying to do his job. The rails where the Maco Light appeared were pulled up, and the light no longer shows up there.

Another famous ghost light has nothing to do with trains. The Brown Mountain Lights have been appearing along their namesake ridge since before written history. Legends abound from the lights. They are told to be the spirits of native maidens searching for the bodies of warriors fallen in a great battle on the ridge, or the light of a dedicated slave, searching for his lost master. The lights appear sporadically, but one possible pattern may be that they appear more likely in the fall, after a rain or light storm. No acceptable theory for the lights has been put forth, though there may be some strange and nebulous cause associated with shifting geologic events and gases or reactive elements.

In addition to these lights are many more. Here are a few, with the locations of some of them provided. Others are so obscure that it is difficult to determine exactly where one might see them.

Cove City Light

Cove City & Trenton   35.18006° -77.31922°

A mysterious light appears to cross the road on the straight stretch of NC 41 between Cove City and Trenton. The light has been known to both follow and go through cars driving down the highway. Legend has it to be the spectral lantern of a mother searching for her baby, who was abducted by a mother bear after the bear's cub was killed.

Ephraim's Light

Seaboard   36.49153° -77.44149°

The ghost light of a slave who was killed after slaying his owner haunts the area around the Woodruff House, somewhere on the outskirts of these coordinates at Seaboard.

Mintz Light

Roseboro   34.89086° -78.48580°

A simple but often told tale by the locals of a bobbing light that appears across the nearby train tracks. It seems to be like the more famous Maco and Vander lights, but with less of a story attached.

Aulander Light

Aulander   36.25604° -77.02758°

Also known as Earley Station Light, there are many tales of this strange ghost light appearing in the woods between the old station and the nearby town of Aulander. The legend is that a train conductor died in an accident on the rails when another train hit his.

Teach's Light

Bath   35.45407° -76.81812°

One of many spots where Blackbeard's ghost is supposed to haunt, Teach's Light was seen as a ball of fire crossing the water from Plum Point, rumored home of Edward Teach, across the water to Archbell Point. Neither place is accessible by land, but the area can be seen from Bath.

If this is not enough, read about the Maco Light, Vander Light, Pactolus Light, and the Brown Mountain Lights in *Did You See That?*

A note on visiting, or more accurately, not visiting these places. Since many of these spots are on rail lines, be aware that it's dangerous to go out where trains are running, especially at night. Who knows who you will run into, or will run into you. And even if there aren't train tracks, some of these spots are on private property. The only one that really might be okay to visit is Brown Mountain, and even then the bugs will swarm you. Just take a flashlight out back and play with the kids, and enjoy the legends.

Open Pit Granite Quarry

Mount Airy   36.50607° -80.58594°

When Robert S. Gilmer wanted to start a farm back in 1849, the one thing he knew he didn't want to grow was rocks. So he was really disappointed when he found a big white rock right in the middle of the land he had just purchased. He was so angry that he demanded his money back for that part of the property.

Because of that, the Mount Airy White Granite Quarry was bought for nothing.

And the granite has been coming out ever since. Getting the granite isn't easy. Granite is a stubborn stone. A block is cut using narrow water jets at 40,000 pounds of pressure every square inch. Afterward, a diamond cable saw separates the bottom of the block from the rest of the granite, and then finally Primacord explosives are used to completely remove the block from the wall of the quarry. The explosives are loud, happening often during the day. Luckily, visitors to the quarry can see these things, and hear the explosions, every day that the quarry is open. There is a viewing area to see the entire operation, open to anyone who wants to drive up and see. The observation area is open during daylight hours every day of the week.

The rest of the quarry is not accessible to visitors due to the dangers involved in running an open quarry, which has to follow the rules any mine would. And it's too bad people can't at least see all the manufacturing going on in the factories nearby. Well, actually, they can see the end products, at least. Mount Airy Granite is a popular choice for curbing up in northern states where softer concrete curbs get eaten up by snow and snow plows. But even more visible might be in the monuments where it has been used. The World War II memorial in Washington, D.C., as well as the Arlington Bridge, are both made with granite from Mount Airy. And closer to home in N.C., the Wright Brothers Monument was built with blocks shipped over from the quarry.

But visitors don't have to even go that far to see the many uses of the granite. Mount Airy was built from the stone. Houses, churches, the local library, banks, and many municipal buildings were all built with granite. The local veterans memorial and the police department both are made from Mount Airy granite. The sheriff's department is not made from granite. Because there is no sheriff's department. Unlike its TV counterpart, Mount Airy does not have a sheriff.

So Mount Airy was built from granite. It was also built on granite, literally. The visible part of The Rock, as locals refer to it, is about 60 acres. But the total amount is much bigger. Granite stretches about seven miles across the land, a swath that is also a mile wide. And the granite runs deep, about 8000 feet down. Dig down a few feet in most places, and the rock will appear. Some houses only have two feet of soil in their yard, and few of the places have basements.

The sheer volume of granite in the quarry means that granite will be coming out of the mine for up to 1000 years.

Oddity ★★

The size of the pit is hard to imagine until it is viewed in person. The white granite gleams out on the quarry, the giant forklifts hustle, and the explosions boom. It is a sight to behold.

Difficulty ★

With the addition of the viewing area, it is very easy to go by to see the quarry. The explosions can be heard often, but not felt, so as not to shake or crack the granite. Go by on a sunny day, and take shades.

The quarry is so big and bright white, with it being surrounded by the dark green forests of Mount Airy, that the mine can actually be seen by astronauts in space.

Gravity Hill

Pooletown   35.58359° -80.24503°

Another of the very popular gravity hills in North Carolina is the Richfield Gravity Hill. Actually located on Richfield Road near Pooletown, the uphill road starts a little ways out of town on a straight uphill track heading south toward Richfield. Near the beginning of the hill is a gravel pull off where people have parked to make sure the road is clear before pulling out. Drivers will stop at a mark on the road, place the car in neutral, take their foot off the brake, and the car quickly begins to coast up the straight road. Up the hill.

The legend tells that a woman in a car with her kids stalled out there on the straight path. Unable to move her car out of the way, she was hit by a truck, killing her and her children. Now any car that is stuck in the road will be pushed up the hill by unseen forces, the ghosts of the mother and her kids, still trying to save others from the same fate they suffered.

The spookiest part is, after cars get pushed up the road, drivers have found handprints on the back of their cars, physical manifestations of the spirits that pushed the car up the road. Some drivers have sprinkled talcum powder on their cars rear decks to see the hand prints appear.

So the legend goes on. The truth? Well if you really want to know... if not, stop reading here and jump in your car.

In reality, gravity hills are very strange optical illusions. The road seems to go uphill based on the way the sides of the road, the land beside it, appear to be sloped. The road actually runs downhill slightly. The easy way to see this is to pour some water on the road and see which way it runs. The hand prints, well, everyone has hand prints on their car. Try washing the car and making sure no one touches it before going up, or down, the hill. And, if you are willing to try this out, make sure that even if you want to prove it really happens, don't turn the car off. Leave the keys in, car running, and transmission in neutral. It makes it easier to steer, brake, and get going if the driver is in danger.

Oddity ★★★

Yes, it may just be an optical illusion, but still, there is just something that doesn't feel right about the place, because you really think you shouldn't be doing this, going uphill against the pull of gravity. It doesn't matter if you understand the process, it's still spooky.

Difficulty ★★★

While drivers don't actually have to get out of their cars to do this, the big thing is the danger involved. The road is a straight and open track, and not highly travelled. But there still can be cars going up and down the road. It would be incredibly easy for someone to come roaring down the road going way too fast. Don't play in the street, and stay in the car, be on the lookout. Keep the engine running, go during the day, use common sense. If you can't do this, if you can't be entirely sure you are safe, just don't go.

There are several Gravity Hills in the state. Read about one in *Did You See That? A GPS Guide to North Carolina's Out of the Ordinary Attractions* that rolls back up an onramp near Mayodan. Another Gravity Hill is listed in this book, near Laurinburg. And if you really want to explore, head up past Thurmond on Highway 21 toward Sparta. Look for a road to the left, Old Highway 21, at 36.37813° - 80.95865°. Drive about half a mile up the road to the end and turn around. The car will coast up the hill in neutral. Or more accurately, it *may* coast up the hill. A lot of people say they haven't had much luck at this one.

Constellation Airplane Fuselage

Alexis 35.40448° -81.14882°

North Carolina is famous for airplanes, certainly. We even put them on our license plates. And more than one airstrip, military base and even a paintball field have jets out front on sticks or sitting around on the ground. But they aren't as common as the old car your neighbor is planning to fix up. Which is kind of what Brian Hicks is planning on doing with the big plane fuselage he's got in his yard.

It's only a fuselage, and only part of that, to boot. Hicks owns (about) the first 53 feet of a Lockheed Constellation. The plane has a serious history, and this specific one has a very special pedigree. The Constellation was the first pressurized commercial airliner, designed by Lockheed for Trans World Airlines at the insistence of Howard Hughes. TWA needed a plane that could fly transcontinental routes. The design of the plane was beautiful, with a long wide wing like that of the P-38 Lightning fighter, as well as a three rudder tail that lowered the overall height of the plane so it would fit in existing hangars. The Connie served in World War II, and then used extensively for commercial passenger travel after the war. It was even the presidential airliner for Dwight Eisenhower, and the first plane to be designated Air Force One. In 1944, a Connie flew into

Wright Field in Ohio to pick up a very special passenger. Orville Wright got on board, noting the large wingspan of the plane was longer than his first flight. Legend has it that Orville even took control of the plane for a short time.

It took an entrance into the jet age to move the Connie into obsolescence. While passengers moved into faster jet airlines, the Constellation was still used as a freight carrier. It was also a popular military plane in the Air Force and Navy. Connies were popular for lugging radar detection systems for long periods of time. They were used to potentially detect the attack of Soviet bombers and missiles. While most were no longer used by the mid-1970s, some were still used for training.

Which brings up the pedigree of the fuselage sitting in Brian Hicks' yard. It was the very last Connie to fly a mission. It was used to represent a Soviet bomber in fleet exercises over the Atlantic Ocean. It last flew in June of 1982.

After its retirement, this particular Connie went to Florence, SC to be part of a display at the Florence Air and Missile Museum. When the airport needed to expand a parking lot, the planes on display all had to go to new homes or face destruction. This plane had already been damaged when a controlled grass fire got out of control and scorched the bottom of the plane. The Connie was sold for its parts to go into other restorations. Hicks, while working with the Carolinas Aviation Museum to get some other planes from the collection, bid on the Connie, but did not win. He then contacted the winner and negotiated to buy just the front part of the fuselage, thinking he wouldn't be able to move more than that on a flatbed truck. He said he ended up paying more for the fuselage than the other guy did for the whole plane.

After getting the fuselage onto his property, Brian has slowly begun the process of restoring the plane, getting instruments bit by bit to rebuild the interior.

Oddity ★★★

It may be hidden in the foliage of the trees around the yard, and it may only be a bit of fuselage, but it certainly looks out of place there. It's like a 1960s space capsule landed in the woods. And honestly, how he got it there, on a big truck, through those small curvy roads...

Difficulty ★★

It can be seen, briefly, from the street. There is no place to pull over on the twisty road if drivers are going east. There is a tiny bit of dirt driveway to a chained off path where cars can stop. Note the No Tresspassing signs; you can't get close to this one.

Woodside Shoe House

Lincolnton 35.46132° -81.28142°

It really is an odd bit of an attraction, this shoe in the yard of the Woodside Plantation. It defies a simple, cute description, and is best seen rather than described. To merely say, "There is a big shoe in the yard," does disservice to this creative children's playhouse in Lincolnton.

The property and main house are part of a plantation, originally belonging to the family of James Pinckney Henderson, who was born there but moved away to later become governor. Of Texas, but still... The ownership changed hands over time and had a rather cute and unique addition made in the form of a shoe house. A doting uncle built the shoe house for the children of the family sometime after the turn of the twentieth century. His attention to detail was amazing. A full sized door allowed entrance to the shoe through the heel, and a set of windows on each side of the shoe light the inside. A tiny door at the toe would let the wee little toes, er, kids, in and out from the front. On one side, a small stepladder leads to the top of the shoe.

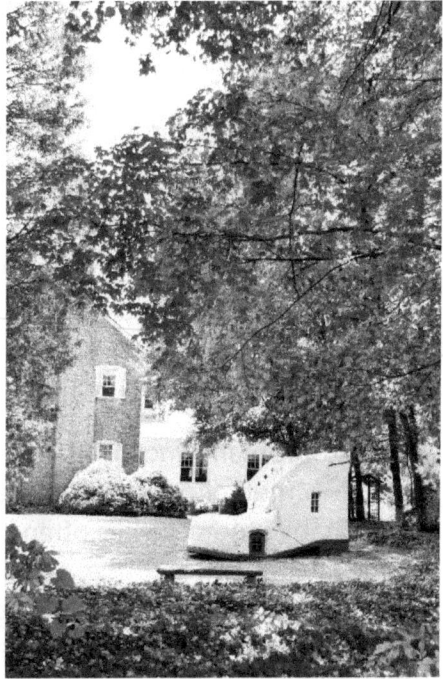

The design predates the Chuck Taylor by decades, but it still is a nice looking high top. A giant lace even hangs from the eyelets.

The shoe house is on private property of Woodside, so visiting and going in the shoe is only done by appointment or when the plantation has an open house. The shoe can easily be seen by the side of the road.

Oddity ★★★★★

Not only is it a strange sight to see a shoe that big in a backyard, but it's doubly impressive to see how nice looking and well cared for it is.

Difficulty ★★

Remember that the property is private, and the road by the house is fairly narrow, with no real pull off. Park in one of the nearby side roads to get out of the way and walk, carefully, to get a picture. But be careful on the side of the road; no one is going to want to be in your shoes if you get in an accident.

The old woman who lived in a shoe, like many old rhymes, is actually a metaphor for other events. While the whole tale's source is debatable, the shoe has often been associated with fertility. Brides would be hit with a shoe on their way to their honeymoon, and shoes would be tied to the back of a car to encourage a family. The old woman "lived in a shoe," meaning she was continually having children, so many she didn't know what to do with them.

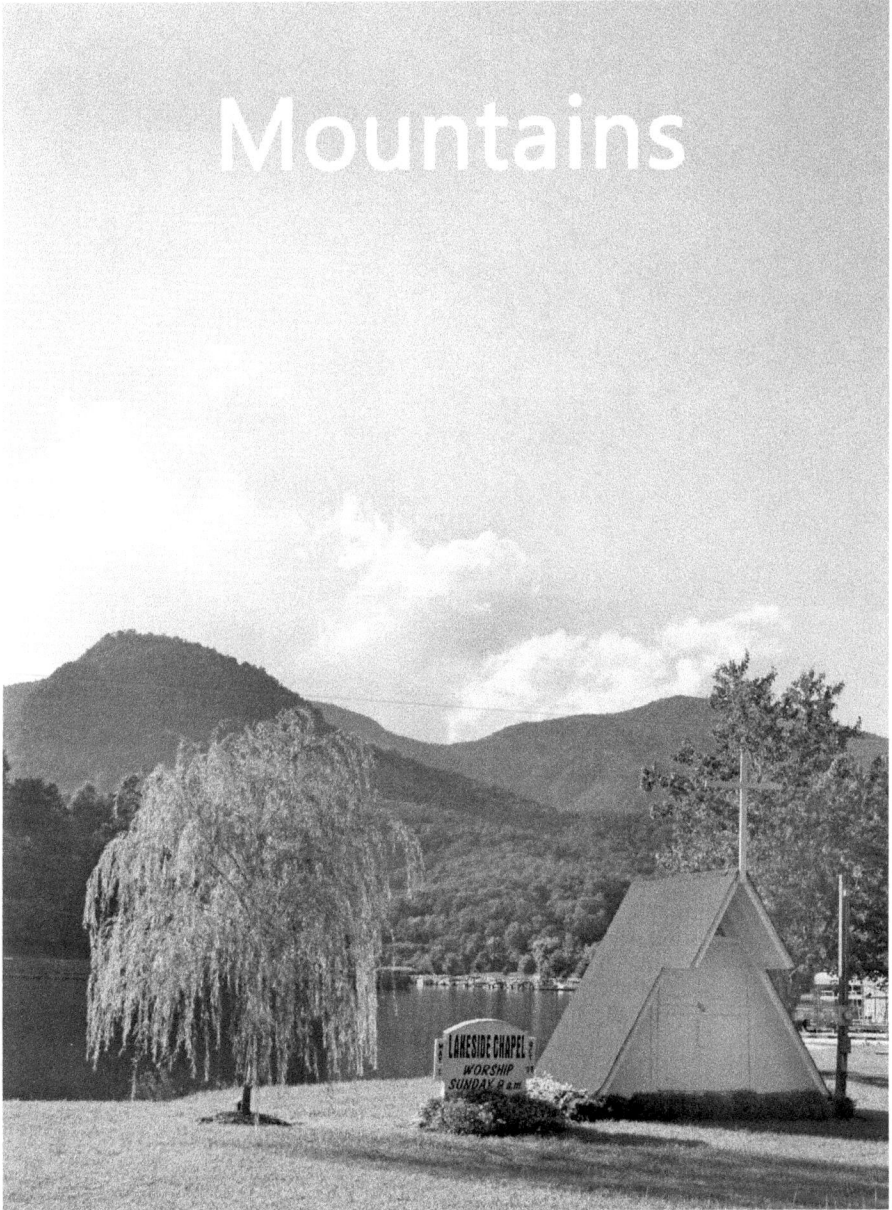

Mountains

Abraham Lincoln Birthplace

Bostic 35.36209° -81.83537°

North Carolina is home to several presidents, only they weren't president when they were home, or they weren't home when they were president. And one president wasn't even born here when he was born here.

Wait, it gets confusing after that part.

The world knows Abraham Lincoln was born on February 12, 1809 in a Kentucky cabin. He was the child of Nancy Hanks Lincoln and Thomas Lincoln, the only one of three siblings to live well into adulthood.

But the town of Bostic, and many in North Carolina, know differently. The big issue is with his mother. Nancy Hanks was probably born by Lucy Hanks, but there has been speculation that she was born out of wedlock, a decidedly juicy tidbit of mud to sling at a political candidate at the time. Here is where legend and oral tales take over. Nancy may, or may not, have been a Nancy Hanks that was placed into servitude to a wealthy plantation owner, Abraham Enloe. Hanks then became pregnant with Enloe's child, and had to leave due to the shame it would bring her. Legends abound at this time. Some tell that it wasn't Enloe at all, that a man named John Calhoun was the possible father. Nancy may have left on her own, spurred on by the Enloe patriarch possibly, or she may have received help. Enloe may have hired a man to take Hanks away, a man of the earth who traveled to rent out land for farming. Allegedly, Thomas Lincoln was hired to take Nancy away to Kentucky. Lincoln traveled with Nancy to Kentucky only after Nancy gave birth in a small cabin near Bostic. Thomas Lincoln would be married to Nancy Hanks in Kentucky by a deacon,

Jesse Head, in 1806. Head would note that Nancy had with her a black headed boy.

Most of this is pure supposition. There very well may have been a Nancy Hanks working for Abraham Enloe in Rutherford County, because there were several women with that name at the time. It can't be determined if she and Abraham Lincoln's mother were one and the same. Furthermore, Abraham Lincoln's age discrepancy of about 5 years, whether born in 1804 or 1809 would be rather noticeable, especially as he aged in school, or went out on his own at 21. Lincoln's father, the recognized one, Thomas, also has been shown to be living in Kentucky all the time he was purported to be in North Carolina, helping Nancy get over the mountains with a baby.

The idea of Lincoln being born in Bostic still nags at believers. But one thing still nags at the believers. Many wish that there was a chance to do DNA tests on descendants of both families, just to be sure.

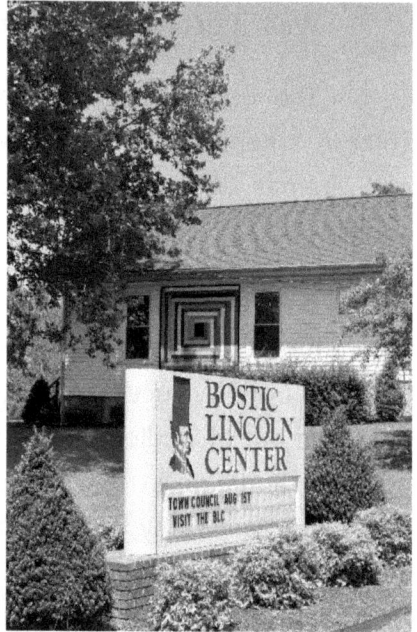

Today, the Bostic Lincoln Center serves as a repository for all speculation of Lincoln's birthright in North Carolina. In addition to some Lincoln memorabilia, there are relics from the remains of the log cabin where Lincoln was purported to be born. Not much remains of the house on Lincoln Hill, near Puzzle Creek just outside of Bostic. But if visitors want to see the site, the only access is through the center.

The Lincoln Center will lead visitors on an easy hike up to see the remaining foundations, as the land is private property, and the Lincoln Center has access to it for tours.

Oddity ★★★

The story is quite strange. Even though there is ample evidence that Lincoln was born in Kentucky, still, looking at Abraham Enloe's descendants, they sometimes look a little similar. And imagine someone with a big hat. Of course, put a big hat on anyone and they will look a bit like Lincoln.

Difficulty ★★★★

The only access to the site is through the Lincoln Center, open only 1-4 on Thursdays, and 10-1 Friday and Saturday. Then you have to make the relatively easy hike to see the foundation and cellar. Admission is free, but you may be able to donate a penny or two, right?

Three presidents were born in North Carolina, but none served as residents. Andrew Jackson was born in a disputed area between North and South Carolina in the Waxhaws region, and served for Tennessee. James Polk was born near Charlotte, in current day Pineville, but served Tennessee as well. Andrew Johnson, who became president after Lincoln's assassination, was born in a log cabin in Raleigh, but moved to, you guessed it, Tennessee.

Flowering Bridge

Lake Lure   35.43572° -82.23436°

It may be true that when a bridge gets built, the first things that happen will be for someone to drive across it, and someone to fish off of it. What usually doesn't happen is for flowers to grow on it. In Lake Lure, that may not have been the first thing to happen on the Rocky Broad River Bridge, but it certainly is the most prolific. Flowers and plants now cover the bridge and the entrance to it, through a dedicated walking path.

The Rocky Broad Bridge was built in 1925, a year before the lake was impounded. It connected the future shoreline of the town of Lake Lure with nearby Chimney Rock and Bat Cave. The narrow span served well for decades, letting people pass over from sleepy Lake Lure into the touristy shops nearby, going for a climb up Chimney Rock, fishing or walking by the Rocky Broad River. The bridge is a three arch span, a simple but elegant design. It reached 155 feet across the gap of the river, but was only 20 feet wide. It may have been fine for narrow cars of the 20s and 30s, but passing a truck going the other way became a somewhat harrowing experience. The state began a replacement bridge, a wide modern span, which was finished in 2011. It sat right next to the old

bridge, the upstart youth turning up its nose at the aging patriarch of the road.

Locals saw the beauty in the bridge, now that it was cleared of traffic. The arches curved gracefully, and the delicate classic lamp posts cast a soft warm glow on the patina of the bridge. The town allowed access to the bridge to build this unique feature, putting an entire flower garden on the bridge's roadway. The garden design was all done locally, mostly by volunteers and local craftsmen. Low walls were put up to contain the soil, and gardeners all pitched in to fill the bridge with flowers and other plants.

Today the bridge and surrounding area are full of greenery. Throughout the bridge there is a meandering path, a swooping curve of a walkway, that lets people take their time as they wander through the bridge. There are several sections of different plants, with native species, exotic plants and carnivorous plants, even fun little novelty flowers that aren't seen very often in most gardens. Interspersed throughout the gardens are decorative pieces of whimsy, little sculptures half hidden by the brush, and other beautiful garden accoutrements.

The walking path is similar to the larger surroundings in a way. The valley of Lake Lure and Chimney Rock is called the Hickory Nut Gorge. It has long been a special and sacred place for the aboriginal people, who used it as a path through the mountains. The ancient highway for natives became, over time, a path for newer visitors to the area to go from place to another. Now the flowering bridge mimics the same path in miniature. People can stroll through, taking their time, seeing all the natural beauty in a microcosm. They still can walk from Lake Lure to Chimney Rock, but they may just want to stop and smell the flowers more often.

Visiting the bridge is relatively easy. It is a short walk from the beach front at Lake Lure, and there is a nice boardwalk path that leads around the lake to the bridge. Mornings and evenings in the summer as best, as the bridge can get hot during the day. There is a lot more to see besides the flowers at the bridge. The lamp posts are new replicas of the originals. The flowers attract loads of hummingbirds, moths, butterflies, bees, and other insects. Visitors might even run into one of the master gardeners that help care for the gardens. Be sure to speak to them, compliment their work, and have them tell of some of their favorite spots.

Oddity ★★

Not weird, so much as incredibly unique. The Lake Lure Flowering Bridge is more than just a garden. The bridge itself is a work of beauty, and the view is different than other places on the lake. It's a great spot for a photo.

Difficulty ★★

Either walk from the beach area or the parking lot at the marina. There is a closer spot near a local coffee shop that allows you to get a cup of joe while you stroll the bridge.

Big Animal Crossing

A Did You See That? Detour

Oversized animals, or oversized anythings, have often been used to attract attention to businesses over the years. From the big muffler men to modern blow up giant gorillas, these things really help attract attention. Even the big wavy guy dancing in the parking lot has his roots in the big statues made in decades past. Animals, and other emblems, were great advertisements. They were easily recognizable, distinguishable from other mascots, and people didn't even need to be able to read to know what they stood for, at least when they were popular.

Now, some companies still do this. They often find a way to zoomorphicize, or take an inanimate object and make it look like an animal, especially if it fits in with their business. Others use giant animals to show off their business talents. Here are a few pretty cool ones to check out on a road trip.

Giant Shark

Snead's Ferry   34.52672° -77.43460°

Shark Attack, a beach store in Snead's Ferry, has an interesting entranceway. A humungous shark opens its mouth to visitors. Even Captain Quint would go back for a bigger boat!

Dinosaur Skeletons

Pikeville 35.48527° -78.05836°

An 18 feet tall, 30 feet long skeletal dinosaur prowls outside Benton & Sons custom fabrication shop. Laser cut from aluminum sheets and assembled on the site, the big Tyrannosaurus has been called "Awesome" by every visitor, young and old, who sees it. And so the name stuck. Awesome the T. rex has recently added a friend, too.

Mercury Cougar

Zebulon 35.82077° -78.33192°

Built in the late 1960s, the big cougar at Howden Classic Cars used to be an advertisement at the Lincoln-Mercury dealership in Raleigh. One of only 4 or 5 left, this one still has some whiskers on it. Ford Motor Company used animals as its code names for the cars it develops; this is why many cars still have animal names. The Mustang originally was called the Cougar during development.

Milk Tank Cows

West Jefferson   36.40253° -81.49118°

Ashe County Cheese has been around, in some form, since 1930. A set of simple, and gigantic, milk tanks sat outside the factory, so in order to beautify the local downtown, local artist Stephen Willingham and some local high school students painted them up and put cow heads on them. No utter thing like it.

Moon Flag Factory

Rhodhiss 35.77163° -81.43243°

Even before cotton was crowned king of the south in 1861, North Carolina was becoming known for its textile production. As early as 1810, North Carolina was making more textiles by hand than Massachusetts was in its mills. It would take over 100 years, but the mills would be built, and North Carolina would be king of the textile mills by the 1920s.

And Rhodhiss would be part of it. Two mills would work on opposite sides of the lake spillway where the dam provided power to the factories. On the northern bank of the waters was a textile mill that made men's clothing, now long gone. The south side was home to the mill that produced synthetic cloth, including the material that would be made into the flags that ended up on the moon for the Apollo landings.

Burlington Industries manufactured nylon material there, coloring the fibers in the factory. The bulk textiles were then sent off to Annin Flagmakers of New Jersey. The flags were ordered through government supply. The flags for the entire Apollo program cost only

$5.50 each, but the pole assembly that was built for the lunar module cost $75 a pop. The poles had to be designed to hold the flag straight out in the vacuum of the moon, where there was no wind to make the flag fly. The flags were stitched with a small sleeve at the top to accept a rod to hold the flag out like a curtain.

Rhodhiss is rightly proud of their small part in the nation's journey to the moon. The town even created a seal showing an astronaut holding one of their flags in honor of the event, and the sign at the city limits proudly displays a space man with the American flag. The mill in town, like many across the state, is now closed and empty. The town hopes to use the building once again, either in a new capacity or for more manufacturing. The mill still stands proud, with beautiful wooden floors and a lot of history.

A curious part of the flags on the moon is that, due to the extreme temperatures and the unfiltered ultraviolet light, the flags probably have all turned completely white. Just like on Earth, the sun takes its toll on fabrics, slowly fading the color from them. In the decades that the flags were exposed to the full force of the sun, they most likely are bleached. It is also highly possible that the flags' material has degraded and turned to ash. One is certain to not be standing. Buzz Aldrin reported that the flag he and Neil Armstrong put up on the moon was blown over when the lunar module blasted off from the surface. Later astronauts made a point to place the poles farther from their landing sites.

Oddity ★

The mill is locked, with its insides hollow, empty, and still. A somewhat sad epitaph, but also very similar to the stark emptiness of the lunar landscape.

Difficulty ★

The view from the mill is beautiful, with the nearby dam and the calm waters of the lake. There is a parking lot in front of the mill, but feel free to take some time to enjoy the rest of the lake. Rhodhiss is even finding a new way to benefit from the views. Visitors might even find a new home to move into.

Witch's Keyhole

Lenoir 35.92719° -81.52512°

North Carolina, and much of the South, really, is ripe with tales of the supernatural. Witches, hoodoos, haunts, and spooks all wander the lands and legends of times past and present. Even in today's modern times, people still whistle through graveyards.

Long ago, witchcraft was even more believable. The whims of nature, good luck, or bad, could all be explained away if a witch caused it. Fishermen knew to leave a dime on the dock of a witch's shack to ensure good weather or a decent catch, and to leave a good fish on the dock when they returned. Kids would keep their distance sometimes, other times they would be rewarded with some change in exchange for a frog or bug. Witches were on the extreme edges of society, doing the deeds that no one else would, and often taking the blame for all the events that happened that no one else understood.

So it wouldn't be surprising if someone blamed a witch for burning his house down. George Powel lost his log cabin to fire sometime in the 1800s, and he blamed witches trapped in his house for the fire. It didn't matter to him that he was living in a wooden tinderbox. It certainly had to be a witch. So, when he built a new house on the property, he incorporated a keyhole design in the side of the house, up into the attic. The belief was that if a witch or spook was trapped inside, they would fly around and go mad, until they set the house on fire to escape. But a witch can squeeze through a keyhole, no problem. Powell simply created a window of sorts for the witch to find easily. The house stood until the 1970s, when the property was used by the local Methodists to build a church. The fact that it never burned was obvious testament to Powell's inventive design.

The church, in the rather welcoming fashion that Methodists are known, kept the brick keyhole. It now sits out front of the church in a small brick stand, a planter in front of the church that doubles as a sign. The witch's keyhole has become a bit of a legend in roadside stopping places, and while a simple thing, it is an important part of the culture of the state.

Oddity ★

It's the story and the preservation that is so great about this one.

Difficulty ⭐

Obviously, going on Sunday morning might mean a bit of traffic. Of course, they probably would welcome any visitors, and Methodists usually have a pot of coffee on every Sunday.

Körner's Folly in Kernersville goes about keeping witches at bay in a little different matter. At the entrance to the house is a witches' corner. It is a small pot where guests would throw a coin. The witch or haint would be distracted by the shiny coin, go to the pot, and the guests could slip into the house, keeping the witch out.

House of Mugs

Collettsville   35.95870° -81.71073°

Starbucks has nothing on this guy.

Avery Sisk started his coffee mug collection with, you guessed it, an oil lamp. (No one said a cabin made of mugs up an old twisty road in the mountains would make sense.) Sisk and his sister Ruby Shook went to a flea market to purchase an antique oil lamp, and ended up with 750 mugs for the rare sum of $15.

"I don't drink coffee."

He decided to nail them up to the back porch of his cabin. His wife, Doris, wasn't sure of this display of mugs until the reporters started taking pictures, and she started getting in the papers. She likes coffee. So the two started collecting coffee mugs. It may be surprising to know how easy it is to get a lot of mugs at flea markets, antique collections, yard sales, and any other place that might have the cups. The nails were donated.

So the mugs went up. And kept going up. First the cabin. Then the porch, then fence, then the... well, then everything else. Sisk put up every mug he could get. He stopped counting at 18,000. He

estimates that there are about 25,000 on display, with another 8,000 to go. The collection may run the gamut from a large number of mundane coffee cups to a few that are incredibly rare. Sisk has a John F. Kennedy presidential mug that is worth some serious money, if only he would sell. He doesn't, presumably because then he would have a clean spot on his cabin. But he does take donations, if only he can find a place to hang them up.

Visiting the House of Mugs is only slightly difficult, but it is out of the way. Collettsville is a tiny little town, and quaint might even be too strong a word for it. It is certainly out of the way for most folks, but for the people that go there, they have a nice spot to slow down some there. There is a nice general store, where visitors can stop for a honey bun and a bit of conversation while they get gas for the car. And driving down Old Johns River Road in the summer will make just about anyone want to stop for a moment to stick their toes in the cool creek. The road is narrow, but paved most of the way, only to turn into a hard packed and smooth clay, with little rocks that can be kicked up.

Nothing that would stress a driver out unless they are in some low slung sports car. Or maybe they didn't have their coffee yet.

Oddity ★★★★★

The Collettsville Mug House has become a serious attraction over the years since Avery Sisk first put the mugs on his cabin. People from all over the world make a trip up the mountain to see it.

Difficulty ★★

While it is just off the road, the trip from Collettsville up Old Johns River Road is a bit twisty, with several one lane bridges to cross. Be careful on those bridges, there's no guardrails. Is it worth the trip? It's a house covered in mugs! Maybe go when it's not raining, make sure you and your car or truck is ready for the trip.

Nearby to the Mug House is the abandoned town of Mortimer. Once a thriving mill town, it was wiped off the face of the earth by a gigantic flood. Only a few remnants of the town are left, but it is now a popular spot for fishing and kayaking. See it at 35.98100° -81.75931°.

Giant Arrowhead

Old Fort   35.62902° -82.18146°

There is more history in Old Fort than there is in the entire United States. Or at least a longer history, considering settlers traveled there before the Declaration of Independence was signed in 1776. Old Fort at one time was just Fort, actually Davidson's Fort, a defended settlement for the protection of soldiers and settlers from the Cherokee, who had sided with the more accommodating British during the Revolutionary War. Cherokee attacks increased in the area, even though the land that was determined off limits to the colonists. Proclamations of sovereignty were often ignored by the settlers. Davidson's Fort was the westernmost part of the nation at the time.

Old Fort continued to be a safe place to stop for decades after. It was a stop off for the trains that would run to Asheville, often dropping people off to stay at the resort hotel near Andrew's Geyser.

It was also the beginning point for adventurers hiking to Catawba Falls. It still is a good stop off for a bathroom break and a fill up on gas before heading up the Blue Ridge. And a great place to stretch the legs, since there are some nice places and things to see even today.

The giant arrowhead in the middle of town is a hard to miss landmark. The rugged and simple design belies a great bit of history. The arrowhead is a 14 and a half feet tall carved piece of pink granite, placed on top of a 15 feet tall base, covered in river rock, and surrounded by a fountain pool. The arrowhead was dedicated in July of 1930, in honor of the settlers of the town and the fort that was built in 1759. During the dedication, members of both the Cherokee and the Catawba tribes were also in attendance. Though originally dedicated to the settlers, the arrowhead later became known as a symbol of the peace between the settlers and the native tribes. The dedication was also the first formal recognition of peace between the Catawba and Cherokee, as they symbolically smoked a peace pipe.

When visitors go to Old Fort today, it may be hard to imagine that 6,000 people came there to see the dedication all those years ago. Now it is a quaint little town that prefers to stay away from the touristy shops and big development. Little more than a main street and some houses, it still is a step back in time. The arrowhead will get people out of the cars and onto the sidewalks. Once out, there is more to see in town. Stop at the old depot, with some nice displays and clean restrooms, or get a bite to eat before piling back in for the big trip up to Asheville.

Oddity ★★

The design of the arrowhead, so big and unwieldy, on top of a rather kitschy base, with the empty pool around it, gives it a real retro feel.

Don't you wonder if there is a giant arrow shaft buried deep in the ground?

Difficulty ★

The arrowhead is right off the road by the Main Street intersection, next to the town depot. There is parking behind the depot. Be careful around those railroad tracks.

Look Homeward Angel Statue

Old Fort 35.63442° -82.17829°

The little town of Old Fort may be nothing more than a stopover before reaching Asheville for many people, but it certainly is a nice little stopover. And if anyone takes their time to actually visit past the stop at a gas station or bathroom break, they will discover some pretty interesting bits of history. Old Fort for a long time was the end of the line for the trains, where the mountains became too twisted and steep to run tracks. It took an act of sheer determination, and several lives, to build the final stretch from Old Fort to Asheville.

Now, those workers may or may not have had the honor of being buried in the sloping hills of Old Fort, but one person certainly has a rather unique grave marker there. A sad reflective angel, resting on her phthisic foot, clutching her heart in grief, looks down on the grave of Hattie McCanless, who died in 1901. The marker towers over the other gravesites, all with the typical headstones that seem to rest sporadically on the town's hillside cemetery.

The grave marker is significant. It probably is one of the angels once owned by author Thomas Wolfe's father, W.O. "William" Wolfe, who owned a funeral and grave monument shop in Asheville. Wolfe the Father actually had owned several angels over time, and had sold them across the mountains. While this angel is not, probably, the specific angel that Thomas Wolfe writes of in his seminal work, *Look Homeward, Angel*, it is one that would have graced his father's shop, and Thomas' eyes.

The Look Homeward Angel statue resides in a cemetery in Hendersonville. It is a touching memorial to a family member, but the story of Hattie McCanless, and how this angel came to be there in Old Fort, is much more interesting. Hattie was the wife of Samuel McCanless, a photographer, and, it turned out, an avid poker player. Once during a game with William Wolfe, Samuel cleaned the sculptor out. Unable to pay up, Wolfe offered the angel statue in lieu of cash. Samuel happily took the statue, a reflective angel carved in Italy, and placed it on his already deceased wife's grave.

As if acquiring a grave marker in a poker game wasn't enough, Samuel traveled out west, then returned to his home and married his second wife, Geneva. Who happened to be Hattie's sister. One time Geneva became angry at her husband, accusing him of not loving her as much as Hattie. She wanted to know why Hattie had a nice gravestone, and she didn't. Geneva not being dead at the time didn't seem to enter into it as much as it should, it seems.

What was in Samuel's heart at the time is unknown, but what is in the grave is. Oddly enough, all three members of this strange marriage permanently rest under the watchful eye of the contemplative angel. Hattie's grave is marked under the angel's base, while Samuel is buried a little lower down, and Geneva even lower down the hill, all next to each other, in unmarked graves.

Oddity ★★★

Watch your step, the McCanless couples, threesome, family(?) all rest at the feet of the angel. The sculpture holds wilted flowers close to her, a sad message of loss for such a beautiful carving.

Difficulty ★★

Cemeteries in the mountains are done a little different. The land has an odd tilt to it, and often the plots need to be slightly flattened. Going up the narrow road is not too difficult, but it is a little steep. The angel is fenced in, and not that tall, but will tower over the other markers.

Another Wolfe angel is located in Bryson City.

Read about Andrews Geyser, a few miles outside of town, in *Did You See That? A GPS Guide to North Carolina's Out of the Ordinary Attractions.*

Weird Graves

A *Did You See That?* Detour

Cemeteries have an undeserved implication of fear and dread, as if all of these resting places may not be so final after all, that the spirits may rise up to grab the unsuspecting visitor on a late night walk through the graveyard. Passersby whistle a tune to keep the demons at bay, or maybe to keep their thoughts occupied from the souls that lay beneath their feet. But those fears are unfounded; all the graves are memorials for the lives that came before them. Some are lives well spent, some reveal a life cut short. But they all help to create a remembrance. When we visit a cemetery, whether it be a family grave site, a church plot, an old nearly abandoned bone orchard, or a single grave, when we visit, we help to keep the history of that person alive, long after they are dead.

North Carolina has a plethora of interesting grave sites. A family plot that once was in the middle of nowhere is now in the middle of a parking lot. Unknown people are now famous because of their graves, or the way they died and were buried. There are some graves that mark only a piece of a person, while another marks, well, several pieces. The dates can tell stories, as can the markers themselves. There are some interesting people buried in some interesting graves along the Tar Heel State, and they have had their final honors turned into some popular tourist spots. Here are a few of the famous, and infamous, grave markers, tombs, cemeteries, marble towns, whatever you may call them, in the state.

Old Burying Ground

Beaufort 34.71810° -76.66395°

This famous and extremely old cemetery is graced with a large number of interesting grave sites. The northeast corner is seemingly empty of graves, because it's the oldest section, with a large number of unmarked graves from the early 1700s. The first marked graves are made with seashells, wood, or brick, as stone was too expensive to bring in. Some tombs are vaulted or covered with brick in order to keep high waters or wild animals from the deceased. Several graves are famous for their uniqueness in some way. A common grave of sailors from the *Crissie Wright* shipwreck are buried there. A British officer died onboard a ship in the harbor, and was buried in full dress uniform, standing up and facing England, saluting his king. Captain Otway Burns, a hero of the War of 1812, is laid to rest in the graveyard. A cannon from his ship was later placed on his tomb. Two little girls, taken too soon, lay resting in the cemetery. Vienna Dill died of scarlet fever, and was buried in a glass topped coffin. Another girl, unknown but for her way of burial, is merely known as the little girl buried in a rum keg. Her father, a ship's captain, had promised his wife to bring her back from England. On board his ship, the girl died, so her father

sealed her in a keg of rum to prevent her remains from decomposing. She was buried in the barrel.

Fort Fisher Hermit Grave

Carolina Beach 34.01790° -77.91464°

Hidden deep in the woods on the soundside of Pleasure Island is the Newton Family Homesite and Cemetery, next to the Federal Point Methodist Church cemetery. When Edward Harrill died, his remains were interred in the Newton family graves. Harrill was better known as the Fort Fisher Hermit, and his life is as well known as the tragedy of his death. The grave is notable for the gifts of seashells and coins in a pan, a donation for Harrill in the afterlife.

Rachael Vinson and George Deans Graves

Goldsboro 35.42491° -77.96952°

The strange set of graves only gives a hint to the weird love story that wasn't. Rachael Vinson was in love, desperately, with George Deans. Sadly, George didn't notice Rachael at all, so Rachael gave in and announced her love to the man. George was nonplussed, and shunned her advances. Her heart broken, Rachael died within a few months. Her lasts words were a pledge to be with George forever in the next life.

George may not have believed it at first, but upon passing her grave at the cemetery, a glowing cloud came down upon him, rendering him unconscious. Upon awakening, he found that he could not use his right hand. He lived alone another 32 years until he was buried in the same cemetery.

The two graves have symbolic messages, and an added spooky bit to one. Rachael's has three flowers, wilting in a hand, a symbol of purity and love that never blossomed. George's shows a functioning right hand, clasping a woman's hand, as a symbol of promise in the cross over from one world to the next. But on the back of George Deans' grave marker has formed a visage of a woman, with a patient look on her face. People who have seen photos of Rachael Vinson swear it looks just like her.

Grave With A Roof

Mount Pleasant   35.33729° -80.44255°

Dr. Solomon Furr was once Lieutenant Solomon Furr of the North Carolina Infantry. After a particularly rainy night, Furr and another soldier made pact that when one of them died, the other would promise to keep their grave dry. When Furr passed away, a tent of wooden shakes was placed over his grave.

Bleeding Tombstone

Mount Pleasant 35.33844°-80.44669°

It's actually a marker honoring Heinrich and Russena Furrer, early settlers of the area. It is said that the stone will bleed during a rainstorm. It's more of an odd natural occurrence, but it's still a famous urban legend.

Elmwood Cemetery

Charlotte 35.23643° -80.84803°

Elmwood is the final home to several North Carolina congressmen and generals, but its more famous residents are known for their markers. Henry Severs has a tomb built from a 15 ton block of granite in the shape of a log cabin. No, he had nothing to do with maple syrup. He was a member of the Woodmen of the World, a fraternal organization that supported families when the principal money earner was injured or lost. Another famous marker is a simple obelisk, except for the elephant on the grave. John King was an elephant trainer who was killed by one of his elephants. His coworkers paid for his gravestone, complete with a carving of the elephant that killed him. Additionally, Elmwood is the final resting place of Randolph Scott, an actor famous for his portrayal of handsome western heroes.

Peter Stuart Ney

Cleveland   35.76082° -80.68423°

The covered grave of school teacher Peter Stuart Ney is rumored to be the actual final resting place of Michel Ney, a marshal in Napoleon's army. Michel Ney was the last French soldier to leave Russia, and named The Bravest of the Brave by Napoleon himself. After Napoleon's return to power and his defeat at Waterloo, Ney was executed and interred near his place of death. But soon after, a man appeared in the U.S. by the name of Peter Stuart Ney. People who fought with Napoleon would often recognize Peter as Marshal Ney. Every time he was recognized, Ney would soon move to a new location. It is said that often when drunk, Peter would admit to being Marshal Ney. On his deathbed, he finally admitted being the famous marshal for Napoleon. His grave is covered by a brick tomb, and a French flag flies over his plot.

World's Heaviest Twins

Hendersonville   35.24525° -82.54754°

After suffering from side effects to the measles, young Billy and Benny McCrary's pituitary glands were damaged, sending their bodies into a massive growth spurt. By high school they were both over 400 pounds, and on their way to surpass the 700 pound mark as adults. Their size made them celebrities, popular as wrestlers as well as just being big guys. The

twins were known to get around on specialized minibikes so that they didn't have to walk as much. Travel was difficult, as they each had to travel in converted heavy duty vehicles to handle their weight. Billy died at 32 from complications of a fall from his bike, while Benny died at 54 of heart failure. Their grave marker in Crab Creek Cemetery sports images of the twins' signature motorcycles.

Charlie Silver's Graves

Kona 35.95127° -82.18455°

In going to the Silver family graves at the old Kona Baptist Church, visitors will notice something different about the grave markers of Charlie Silver. There are three of them, or four. We'll go with four. A large marker shows Charlie's name, while three smaller rectangles with the initials C.S. on them. And that begins the gory and sad story of Charlie Silver and his child bride Frankie Stewart Silver.

It begins quickly with beautiful young 14 year old Frankie married to 17 year old Charlie, who have a child soon after. About a year into family life, Charlie begins drinking and possibly abusing Frankie, and the young mother fears for herself and her baby. Then Charlie goes missing. But bits of oily ash and bone were found in and around the cabin, and a pool of blood had dripped down between the slats into the ground below. Frankie had bludgeoned Charlie and chopped him up, hiding the body parts to disguise the crime. Since his body parts were being discovered at different times, they were also buried at different times.

Poor Frankie didn't fare nearly as well. After being found guilty of Charlie's murder, she was hanged in Morganton. The combination of a little girl being hanged and the building of a legend led to Frankie getting the dubious honor of being the first woman hanged in North Carolina. While this isn't true, she probably was the first woman hanged in Burke County. Her father intended to bury her in the family plot, but the heat took its toll on her remains. Her father purportedly buried her in an unmarked grave behind a tavern. Today a marker where her grave may or may not be is on private property outside of Morganton.

There are plenty of other unique graves in North Carolina. Read about the unidentified sailors buried on the coast in *Did You See That? On The Outer Banks*. And read the tragic tale of Tom "Dooley" Dula in *Did You See That? A GPS Guide to North Carolina's Out of the Ordinary Attractions*.

Swinging Foot Bridges

Mitchell & Yancey Counties

36.04360° -82.22530° (Oldest swinging bridge in the state)

36.00744° -82.24669° (Straddles Yancey & Mitchell County line)

A bridge is more than an architectural thing. It is a conduit from one land to another.

The bridges of Mitchell and Yancey counties have straddled the rivers and creeks of the rolling mountainous lands for decades. The create connections where there would only be shouting distances, and link people to roads, people to stores and schools, and people to people. For such simple little things, they have been incredibly important to the people that live there.

Spanning a river or creek has never actually been hard. Long ago it would only take some boards or a few logs to help get across the water. Some traverses were simply created to keep feet dry. Others were made to help span deep water that normally wouldn't be able to cross. Of course, the biggest reason that there was a bridge built across a river was because there was something important on the other side. Or sometimes it was someone.

The suspension bridges in the mountains were first built in the late 1800s. Usually using local scrap materials, it was simple to put up some poles and run a rope or cable with suspenders down to hold some scavenged planks up over the river. All the original bridges wore out, whether due to second rate construction, or river floods and storms. The State Bridge Maintenance Unit took over the building and repair of these paths in 1947. Now the Division of Transportation manages the bridges, with 21 different suspension footbridges in 6 counties of the mountains.

The bridges meant a lot to the people that lived in these areas. They allowed access to school for kids, even in the winter when the wind blew cold over the river. In the summer it meant a lazy spot to sit and watch the water roll by, while children dangled their feet over the side and chucked rocks into the stream. For adults it made the daily routines a little easier, when the store or the church was on the other side of the river. And more than one person would meet another on opposite sides of the river due to these bridges. Two people would become one couple because of a shortcut over the river. No matter how bouncy or unstable, it was probably worth it for a young man to go cross the bridge to go courting the beautiful woman across the creek.

Today the bridges are maintained by the DOT, though still with a lot of simple charm. The bridges still bounce, the walkways are still wood, and the rivers still rush underneath. The bridges still link two lands together. Some just go across the river, while others lead to roads that lead to somewhere else. There are 13 bridges in Yancey and Mitchell counties alone. Only some are accessible from a more main road. While some are part of trails and walkways, most still serve their original purpose. The two listed with coordinates are both popular to visit, historic, and accessible.

Oddity ★★

The reason behind the bridges is rather mundane, as it is for most bridges, to get from one place to another more easily. Walking on one gets a little odder. The wood bounces, the cables stretch, you can see right down, down to the rocks and water below. There are signs that warn the capacity of the bridges is 4 persons, but is that 4 kids, adults, just an average? What do you do if you meet someone coming the other way? What if that kid starts bouncing up and down?

Difficulty ★★

Seeing them merely means a trip through some nice twisty backroads, but to walk across, you have to get out and take that first step. Once you feel the spring and sway of the bridge, the second step is up to you to decide. Be careful.

Lost Cove

Near Ramseytown   36.06646° -82.39052°

It is not surprising that a secluded valley, long lost to time, with no real access to it, would be called Lost Cove. The name has a wonderful appeal, a haunting Bali Hai like calling, a mythical Shangri-La hidden deep within the tall mountains and sheer cliffs of the Appalachians. But Lost Cove is real, as real as the history it still holds, even if the last residents left decades ago.

Nestled into the valley of the sheer faces of Flattop and Unaka Mountains, with the Nolichucky River bounding the land to the north and west as it rolls through the cliffs, Lost Cove was founded sometime before the Civil War. The first settlers may have been drawn by the streams and meadows, but the isolation and proximity to the border with Tennessee may have had something to do with it, too. Rumors tell of members of Daniel Boone's party settling the land, as well as moonshiners liking the isolation of the cove. A moonshiner from the area was once brought up to the nearby magistrate. The judge threw out the case, saying he didn't have jurisdiction over the area. The disputed border made Lost Cove popular with moonshiners due to the safety from the law, as well as the relative privacy. Soon the land became populated and self sufficient.

Like most places that get popular, something happens to mess things up. This time it was the railroad that ruined paradise, though it wasn't so bad at first. With logging in the area flourishing, the rail lines came in, following the river, to haul out the trees cut from the cove and over the hills. When the trees and the logging industry ended, so did the visits from the trains. With no easy ability to get in and out, as well as no way to deliver supplies to the little village, Lost Cove declined. The last resident of Lost Cove left in 1957.

After that time, the remains of the town went into the decline typical of ghost towns abandoned to nature. A tin roofed house still sits in the forest, home to only memories of the family that once lived there. A church, now no longer standing, graced the the town, and a school served the children for most of the rest of the week. The school is mostly overgrown now. Scattered throughout the ghost town is the detritus of a community that worked the lands. Tools, a few chimneys, stone walls, even an old car chassis are partially hidden in the overgrowth. And, with all life, even in a small town like this, there is a cemetery, sitting atop a relatively open knoll. One can imagine the villagers finding the easiest spot for their ancestors to rise up to heaven.

Farther along from the ghost town is another trail, though difficult and rocky, which leads to a narrow overlook to the Nolichucky River. The broad river flows relentlessly, and sometimes floods. Along the banks runs the railroad line, with trains still passing by every day. Passing, but no longer stopping.

Getting to Lost Cove is difficult to say the least. It is only accessible by hiking in, and then hiking out. There has been one trail that leads to Lost Cove for a while, appropriately named the Lost Cove Trail. It is a steep hike, begun at a gravel parking lot hidden deep within the woods at the base of the mountains. Turn off highway 19W onto Howell Branch Road and go until the road forks, taking the gravel road to the left at

36.04416° -82.35822° Howell Branch Fork

This is a twisty, tight, gravel and dirt road. If you continue up this road, make sure you have a vehicle that can safely get up the mountain, handle the roads, and that the driver has the skill to drive up to the parking lot, at

36.05452° -82.37834° Lost Cove Trail Parking Lot

From the parking lot, the rest of the way is on foot. There is the beginning of a trailhead that leads from the parking lot straight up the hillside, which will lead into an open plain called Joe Lewis Field. West of there at the top of the ridgeline will be a narrow, unmarked trail that is usually kept mowed to designate it as a path. This will lead to the more worn Lost Cove Trail. Follow the trail to reach the remnants of the ghost town, where you may (or may not) find the few remaining parts of the town, including the house, school, and the cemetery. The old graveyard is located at the far end at around 36.06782° -82.39344°.

Now, how much warning and disclaimer does the visitor need? Really? To begin with, even the road is a bit in the middle of nowhere, so there isn't going to be a nearby gas station or hotel to serve the wants of the casual traveler. The road to the parking lot is gravel and twisted. The hike to Lost Cove is, on average, two and a half hours (!). And it's a bit of a climb, with a lot of elevation changes. Once there, expect to spend at least an hour in the old town, plus more if you want to hike to see the river. Then you have to go back, which will take probably more than two and a half hours, because you are already tired. So, considering anyone trying this will need 6+ hours of hiking time, with all the supplies, food and water, first aid, all the stuff you need to pack in and out on your own (no, there are no bathrooms up there), this should only be undertaken by knowledgeable experienced hikers who understand not only how to get around in the outdoors, but know how to prepare by checking the long term weather and to check in with people to keep safe.

There has been a new addition to the trail to Lost Cove recently. The Devil's Creek Trail connects with the Lost Cove Trail. Even though it is about twice as long, the Devil's Creek Trail is somewhat flatter, so there is less elevation change. Either way, you are in for a hike.

Oddity ★★★

Lost Cove has become legendary as a ghost town, mentioned among hikers in awe across the east coast. The old town has over a hundred years of history, and has been abandoned for over half a century.

Difficulty ★★★★★

Unless you have already done big hikes and know how to spend the entire day, and maybe a night, outside in nature, just don't go. You need to be ready to do this physically, with hiking shoes, clothes, a pack, full supplies, and a couple of other people at least to keep you safe. Do you own a hand held GPS unit, one that isn't attached to your phone? Do you know how to use it? Do you use it regularly? If you answered no to any of this, don't go.

The land in and around Lost Cove was purchased by the Southern Appalachians Highlands Conservancy. The SAHC is a nonprofit that protects the land of the area for residents and visitors, as well as animals and plants, to enjoy now and in the future. So pick up that trash, you!

Paint Rock

Paint Rock   35.94474° -82.89846°

Decorated onto a cliff face next to a gorge cut into the mountain wall, a path that had been used by travelers since prehistoric times, are some of the most famous and oldest of pictographs in North Carolina. Paint Rock has been famous for centuries by the explorers and visitors to the area. It was documented as early as 1796, and was mentioned by John Strother in his 1799 diary when he was surveying the border of North Carolina and Tennessee.

But in truth it was known even longer than that. Tests to the paint show that the marks, rectilinear stripes of orange and yellow, are over 5,000 years old. There were even more painted decorations along the rock wall, but many have become lost or obscured over time. The wall area was long a stopping point for travelers, as the gorge was about the only way to easily get through the mountains without going over them. Travelers would stop there and camp, burning tree stumps for firewood and creating soot plumes that coated the walls and covered the lower designs. There may have been paintings of people and animals in addition to the patterns painted on the wall, but they are long gone, lost by the damage of fire, and the wear and tear of weather.

Now only a small part of the original design is still visible. The stripes may have been made by natives to the area. It is likely that the native tribes used the nearby hot springs as a healing treatment, even seeing them as having mystical power. The pictographs may be a type of tribute to the springs, a ritual to honor their use by the aboriginals. They may have merely been nothing more than a traffic sign of sorts, to recognize that they were on their way to the springs. And considering the amount of more modern graffiti nearby, they may have been made out of boredom, though making the paints would have meant at least a minimum of care in the artwork put on the cliff wall.

Paint Rock can be seen by driving up River Road from Hot Springs. Oddly enough, the town of Paint Rock is on the other side of the French Broad River and there is no access to Paint Rock from that side. The cliff of Paint Rock is right on the North Carolina/Tennessee border, right before the dirt road turns up into the gorge. There are some small parking areas along the sides of the narrow road to pull over. Seeing the painted marks requires some searching, and binoculars or a telephoto lens will help. What will help the most is to go during the day, when the sun is out. As shade hits the wall, the pictographs disappear, and they are generally hard to find anyway. The pictures are about 150 feet before the turn into the gorge, and about 30 feet up. Look for wavy sets of lines hidden in a small alcove. There is a slight overhang that protects the paintings from the weather, which has helped preserve them over the millennia.

Once you find them, head back into town for a soak.

Oddity ★★

Finding and seeing the pictographs is difficult even if you know when and where to look. Timing is everything on this. But once seen, it is a great tick in the book of the rare and wonderful part of the state that you can say you have seen.

Difficulty ★★

River Road starts out as a nice paved road with lots of pretty little houses and a view of the river. It turns into a gravel road, though still fairly smooth, as drivers head toward Paint Rock. It may get paved soon, as it heads into Tennessee. The road on the TN side is paved but very narrow. Care should always be taken on any gravel road, especially near a river, and especially if it is raining. Or snowing. Or sleeting, or... well, you should just know better by now than to drive when it's not safe, right?

World's Largest Quilt and Bed

Franklin   35.16221° -83.31571°

It gets cold in the mountains during the wintertime. So it's not surprising that Franklin is the quilting center of the state. Its multiple quilt shops and guilds make it a haven for people who found the hobby, and may have turned quilting into more of an obsession. But they do stay warm!

Quilting is an ancient art, done for thousands of years. Essentially, a quilt consists of three layers, with a soft base, a middle batting to make the quilt warm, and a more decorative top layer. Early American quilts were single fabric pieces, with one big cloth sewn on top of the batting, then decorated with needlework. It wasn't until the nineteenth century that patchwork quilts became more commonplace. Originally, the patchwork quilt let the makers use up all the extra scraps of cloth used for other purposes, not wasting the material. The finished quilt may or may not have had a pattern of the pieces, but it would have pieces of cloth that would also appear on a family's clothing, perhaps lending a sense of souvenir to the quilt. A sort of early precursor to the t-shirt quilt of today. The patchwork quilt soon became an object of the talent of the quilter. The patchwork became a pattern, and the task became harder and more skillful, until the quilt became a complex and impressive art form.

Like the t-shirt quilt, there are other types of quilts that help tell a story. Families do quilts together, each person doing one square to represent part of the family life and history. This not only preserves some of the family history, but also allows children to be taught lessons in sewing and quilt making. Quilters even get together to make a quilt in a group, where each person adds one square. These were some of the reasons for the formation of Maco Crafts, a cooperative formed from the Macon Program for Progress, which was a local community group formed in the 1970s to help Macon County residents with training and improving their life skills. Maco Crafts helped train people in crafts, especially quilting, making Franklin and the area well known for the quality of their quilts. In 1982, as part of an exhibition for the Knoxville, TN, world's fair, the group got together to create the world's largest quilt. It is a monstrous 19 by 22 feet big, large enough that it was even hung outside on an old fire watchtower to fully display its enormous length. It contains 116 quilt squares, done by different members of the Maco Crafts group, as well as a larger square with the group's name on it.

Not to be outdone, the woodworker's group in Maco Crafts built the world's largest bed.

Both bed and quilt have been on display at the Whistle Stop Mall in Franklin, though occasionally the quilt would be out on display at other locations. Considering the number of movers needed to relocate the bed, it usually stays in place. However, the Whistle Stop Mall has a new (as of this writing) location, and the quilt and bed may be in storage at some times. Or there might be someone sleeping in it. Or there might be twenty people sleeping in it. At least they will be warm.

Oddity ★★★

The quilt is no longer the largest in the world, with larger ones being made that are so big they can't be regularly displayed. And those usually must be temporarily stitched together, then taken apart to be stored. This quilt is a true quilt, made by one group. The bed is equally impressive, even though no one makes a mattress for it.

Difficulty ★

Whistle Stop Mall will normally have these on display during business hours, and there is often a lot of other interesting things to see there. The old store with its façade was impressive to see. The new place will be equally interesting. It might be a good idea to call before going to check on the quilt and the hours available.

North Carolina has more than the world's largest quilt. There are also quilt trails throughout the state, where quilt blocks have been painted onto displays to hang on businesses and buildings. Read more about the Quilt Trail in *Did You See That? A GPS Guide to North Carolina's Out of the Ordinary Attractions*.

More Did You See That? Detours

There are always more things to find that can fit in a book. Some places are slowly disappearing. Others are new, but with no big story to them. These are just a few of the many little spots that adventurous folk may want to pass by along the way. Good hunting, all you roadrunners!

Oldest Shipwreck

Hatteras   35.20627° -75.70409°

The oldest shipwreck ever discovered in North Carolina was found on the beach in Corolla. It was covered and uncovered before being first moved to the lighthouse in Corolla, then down to the Graveyard of the Atlantic Museum in Hatteras. It is not currently being restored and may be falling apart. It probably is the *HMS John*, sunk in 1658.

Tregembo Animal Zoo

Wilmington   34.12746° -77.89830°

It used to be the Tote'Em In Zoo, and still has the big stylized lion head entrance there. Supposedly it had the inspiration for The Lion King at one time. The place was notorious for sad animals in cages and the weirdest gift shop on the coast.

Prison Bricks

Raleigh   35.78310° -78.63554°

The bricks in the third governor's mansion to be built in Raleigh were made locally by prison labor. Many of the bricks in the sidewalks have the names of the prisoners that made them written into the clay.

Metal Family Statues

Haw River   36.096739° -79.36880°

This strange family, and the family tractor, often get painted up for different seasons. Easy to see, but the busy road makes it tough to pull over. Just wave and say hi, then keep going.

Old Park Rides

Mt. Airy   36.48849° -80.68053°

Honestly... no clue. It's a collection of older park rides and signs. Is it on private property? Part of a development? Who knows...

Two Story Wendy's

Boone   36.20518° -81.66942°

It may not look that odd, but it's the only two story Wendy's in the world.

Guns 'n Roses

Asheville   35.58298° -82.58517°

A newer statue of a man riding either a pig or a dog, it seems no one can decide, has become quite popular recently. The statue, that is. Not riding pig-dogs. It was made by Dewayne Barton for a metal shop and moved to the Burton Street Community Peace Gardens. Parking is difficult at best.

Asheville Velodrome

Asheville   35.56575° -82.58114°

Also known as the "Mellowdrome," the Asheville velodrome is a bike course that used to be the Asheville Motor Speedway. Bits of the old track and walls are still visible.

Afterword

This was an interesting book for me to write. Not just interesting in the usual way, where I discover new places and the bits of history that go along with them, but also in my expectations changed throughout the book, and how different it was than the first one. I started this book by finding the old Hattadare Indian Park. It was a place that I really wanted to see, because I heard it was slowly fading to nothing, being overtaken by the woods. But in the four years since I first heard of it, the place had been cleaned up, and it looked pretty nice. It felt good to see a change for the better, and it was a promising start to my explorations.

I was also happy to find new places and things. Not just new as in, hey, I didn't know about that, but new as in just made. These places didn't exist when I wrote my first book. The big aluminum dinosaurs were a sight to see.

What else changed? Well, in the time between books, I got rid of the little car, and used the big car for trips. I found that I liked traveling in style and comfort more than having the top down, sometimes. I also found that I didn't like being away from home as much. I did some serious road running on this trip, hitting several spots in a day or two. I also ended up talking with people for hours. There were trips where I really wanted to get going from spot to spot, not stopping long, but then I would meet someone, and we would talk, and the stories would come out. I learned quickly that it was worth the time to listen. There are a lot of people out there with something to say. I enjoyed the talks, folks.

But now I'm done. I'm happy, I'm tired, I'm a little strained at looking at the screen for way too long, but I think I got a fun book done. It's different than the first one, certainly. Some of the spots are weirder, some more obscure. The list of places has gotten a little fuller now, but is by no means complete.

So it is time for a rest, spend some time with the family, let you readers get out there and do some exploring. Who knows what you'll find?

Good Hunting,
Joe Sledge *Aug 2016*

Acknowledgements

Books like this are never the work of one person. I was happy to meet so many people who were knowledgeable on the subjects about which I wrote. They gave me lots of unique information that I could have never discovered on my own. To them I owe my thanks.

Captain Scott Martin for all the help on information about Windy Point and the Fountain of Youth. Alice Butler for putting me on the path for Mintz Light. John Meyer and Lori Harris for information on the Rotary Wheel. Charles Boyett for the history on the Edenton tea pot. Anthony Wilson of Loafers Glory Rafting and Tubing for locations of some of the old swinging bridges. Ralph Petterson for putting me close to the Connie fuselage out in the middle of nowhere. Erik Farrell with the Queen Anne's Revenge Conservation Lab on history of the Voice of America buildings. Chris Hocker at Strange Carolinas for telling me about the places he went that I hadn't been to yet. Rebecca Taylor with Federal Point History for directions to the old Dow Bromine plant. Steve Edgerton of Countryside Retirement Village for the great story on the coffee pot. And a big thanks to my brothers, John, Bob, and Bill, all wealths of historically useless knowledge, just like me, only from farther back. I could always count on them to know of something from before my time. My father, Dr. John Sledge, a wealth of more useful knowledge, gave me a lot of good history to build upon, and my mom, Joyce Sledge, always seemed to know that little bit of color that would spice up a story just so.

Finally, very special thanks to my wife Michelle, who kept me on task, and my patient daughter, who put up with the hours and days I spent writing.

Photo Credits

A very special thanks goes out to all the photographers who let me use their pictures in my book. Sometimes it is just impossible for me to get to a place at the right time, or at all, in a few cases. Sharing your work is a wonderful act. All of you who allow free use of photos though public domain or creative commons are allowing more and more people to see the greater world. Photos are by Joe Sledge unless otherwise noted. All photos are covered under the copyright at the beginning of the book. Usage by permission and does not constitute any endorsement of this work. Some photos were adapted for size, color, or conversion to black & white.

Frying Pan Tower – Richard Neal, Frying Pan Tower

Ethyl Dow Bromine Plant – courtesy of the Federal Point Historical Preservation Society

Rotary Wheel – Wilmington Rotary Club

Fountain of Youth – Capt. Scott Martin

Kindred Spirit Mailbox – Zack Rudisin (CC)

Three Sisters Swamp – Dan Griffin, courtesy of The Nature Conservancy

Wash Woods Station – Twiddy Realty

Dog Track – Public Domain

Tea Pot – John Sledge, Jr.

Megalodon Tooth – Public Domain

Coats Bell Collection – Teresa Overby

Gourd Museum – Teresa Overby

Hester Tire – Gary Dincher (CC)

Boar's Nest – Tracey Duke

Goat Island Bridge – Manuel Turner

Granite Quarry – bobistraveling (CC)

Swinging Bridge – Gary Peeples/USFWS (CC)

Lost Cove – Brenda J. Wiley

World's Largest Quilt – Bob Scott, courtesy of Jean Gregory Evans

Several photos have been placed under use through Creative Commons, which allows for various uses through specific licenses, including the ability to adapt photos. Some have been converted to black and white and adjusted for layout. The licenses may be found at the following web sites.

creativecommons.org/licenses/by/2.0/

creativecommons.org/licenses/by-sa/3.0/

Further Sources

There is always more to discover and more to read than I can comfortably put in one book. Here are several sources for more information about some of the chapters in this book.

To visit Frying Pan Tower, go to www.fptower.com

More information about the Ethyl Dow bromine plant and federal Point can be found at federal-point-history.org

The history of the Wilmington Rotary Club, including the Rotary Wheel park, is at wilmingtonrotaryclub.org

Plan your 18 hole visit to Farmstead Golf Links, including that looong last hole, at farmsteadgolflinks.com

Explore Windy Point, Holden Beach, and the Intracoastal Waterway with Captain Scott at wpnadv.com

Find out what activities are happening at the old pontoon bridge at Sunset beach at www.oldbridgepreservationsociety.org

Want to visit Corolla and the open beaches of the Currituck Outer Banks? Try www.twiddy.com

Visit the Voice of America site and see some of Blackbeard's ship, the *Queen Anne's Revenge*, at www.qaronline.org

See what is happening at historic Glencoe Mill and when it's open at www.textileheritagemuseum.org

Want to see the swinging bridges from a different view? Try www.loafersgloryrafting.com

About the Author

Joe Sledge is a North Carolina native and a graduate of the University of North Carolina at Chapel Hill, where he developed a love for exploring. An Outer Banks local, Joe traveled across the country and lived in Monterey, CA, where he married his wife, Michelle. After ten years on the west coast, they moved back to North Carolina and currently live in the Piedmont, with their daughter. Joe worked for nine years as a special education teacher before beginning his writing with *Did You See That? A GPS Guide to North Carolina's Out of the Ordinary Attractions.*

Notes